JEFFREY VEEN

The Art & Science of Web Design

New Riders

201 W. 103rd Street
Indianap

The Art & Science of Web Design

International Standard Book Number: 0-7897-2370-0

Library of Congress Catalog Card Number: 99-069020

Printed in the United States of America

First Printing: December, 2000

03   02   01   00   4   3   2   1

Trademarks

Warning and Disclaimer

Executive Editor, Karen Whitehouse

Acquisitions Editor, Michael Nolan

Development/Technical Editor, Steven Champeon

Interior Design & Production, Douglas Bowman

Indexing, Aamir Burki

Proofreading, Victoria Elzey

Cover, Jeffrey Veen

Cover Image, Wendy Skratt

For everyone who has ever looked at the Web and asked "Why?" rather than "How?"

Contents

Acknowledgments

*"If I have seen farther than others, it is because
I was standing on the shoulders of giants."*
— Isaac Newton, 1676

This book would not have been possible without years of collaboration with some of the most talented people in the industry. Specifically, I am eternally grateful to have had the opportunity to work with HotWired's creative director Barbara Kuhr. Not only did she spark many of the theories and processes in this book, but she put together an unbelievably competent and articulate design team. Two of those designers in particular, Eric Eaton and Douglas Bowman, have been indispensable sources of inspiration. Doug also designed this book, and spent long hours making sure every detail was perfect.

I'm also thankful that I was able to convince Steven Champeon to edit this book. He suffered through countless iterations and desperate phone calls when I couldn't find the words for the ideas I had. He has inspired much of this work, and has pointed me in the right direction on matters of small-batch bourbon and alternative country music.

The folks at New Riders have been a joy to work with. Michael Nolan and Karen Whitehouse encouraged me to take on this project and pushed me to make it the best it could be. They also took me out to dinner a lot, which really helps.

I also had many, many conversations during the writing of this book that helped to make it what it is. Among those whose opinion I value are Joel Truher, Peter Merholz, Taylor, Tim Gasperak, Christina Wodke, Jon Littell, Drue Miller, Steven Johnson, Mike Kuniavsky, Nadav Savio, Jonathan Louie, Lance Arthur, John Shiple, Jesse James Garret, Alex Wright, Margaret Gould Stewart, Michael Kay, Kim Ladin, Frank Leahy, Dave Hendry, Michael Sippey, Greg Veen, Mark Hurst, June Cohen, David Reid, Jeffrey Zeldman, Derek Powazek, and a bunch of others whose names I've undoubtedly missed.

Finally, none of this would have ever been possible without the unrelenting support and encouragement of my wife Leslie. Thank you for reading chapter after chapter, telling me when things were good *and* bad, and not letting me drop out of school all those years ago.

Introduction

He is well-dressed, confident, standing before the staff meeting ready to present a "revolutionary change in how we view this company's very identity." The conference room lights are dimmed and the LCD projector is humming. Someone types a URL into the 20 square feet of browser on the screen, and up pops one of those sites. "Loading..." the screen reports, and there's a bit of nervous chatter in the room as half a meg of multimedia streams through the corporate T1. Suddenly the screen explodes into spinning text and bright-colored objects careening onto the page. A techno music loop thumps along as executives around the table lean in. "This is," says the proud presenter, "EXACTLY what we should be doing online!"

"Actually," you shout over the maddening music, "this is the LAST thing we should EVER do with our online presence." The music stops. The room is silent but for the slight creaking noise of 16 leather conference room chairs all swiveling in unison to look at you, the Web Designer. You're on.

The skills it takes to be successful on the Web reach far beyond knowing the code. While most of us who build the Web for a living have the basic technologies wired to our brainstem, rare is the designer that fundamentally understands the Web at its core. Yes, there are plenty of resources available to teach us HTML and Cascading Stylesheets and JavaScript and even User-Centered Design. But lacking is a guide to fully understanding *why* the technologies work the way they do, and how to exploit that knowledge to build successful sites.

Back at the conference table, you pause for a moment, then stand up and walk to the screen, pointing out a dozen reasons why this particular site fails—not only as an example of smart Web design, but how it fails to meet the basic needs of your customers. The Web is post-cool now, you slyly suggest. It's time we build a site that pushes our company into a new medium, rather than dragging the baggage of the old with us.

This book is not a reference manual or even a style guide. Rather, it a mentor for Web designers or those wishing to be, whispering in their ears during those meetings. It embodies that nagging voice in the back of your heads while sitting at the screen pushing the pixels around, reminding us that there are now new rules and new ways to break them. It is the college English professor who not only taught you how to write, but helped you to recognize and seek out elegant writing. "You know grammar, you know how to spell," she told you. "Now, let's tear into the classics, let's dig down to the deepest etymologies—this is linguistics for the sheer joy of language and story."

The book is structured around the basic Web concepts that so often get only a passing mention in the reference books on designers' shelves today. Yet these are the very issues Web designers and developers deal with each day.

- How does our Web team work together—we've got marketing writing content, designers laying out pages, and engineers wiring all of it together. Is this the right way to be structured?
- Do I really need to know HTML? Can't I just get by with a good authoring tool?
- How do I incorporate advertising effectively in my site? Will we ever make a dime on this Web investment?
- Everyone is talking about "personalization" and "one-to-one" marketing, exactly what does that mean to you when sketching out a site?
- Our site looks great, until the CEO gets a WebTV for Christmas. Now our vacation is cut short while we rethink our entire design strategy. What went wrong?

- There are so many new technologies vying for our attention. How can I ensure we don't commit our Web site to one, or get stuck designing 3D fly-throughs of the corporate campus?
- We hired a designer, but he works in Photoshop all day and makes us build the pages. We're pretty sure he doesn't even understand HTML. That's not good design, is it?

It seems almost cliché these days to be nostalgic for technology from days past, but I must admit I am. My past is one shared by almost everyone with whom I consider a peer: early video games in elementary school, a Commodore 64 in junior high, and a Macintosh in college. I bring this up because there was a sensation I felt the first time I used a Mac in the dark basement lab at my alma matter. It was a feeling of being disconnected and empowered at the same time. I poked at the elegant icons with my mouse and dragged windows around the screen. "Oh I get it. You don't write programs with this, you just use them!" I suddenly realized that most people would want to use a computer to simply get stuff done. Computers were tools. Very powerful ones, at that.

So here we are, a decade later, facing an explodingly popular World Wide Web. It's disconnection and empowerment all over again. From the initial pit in your stomach: "I can't believe there's so much here!" to the first realization of participation: "I can add to it!" The Web grabs us and draws us in.

The Web is everywhere now. The Web has infused itself into our mainstream culture. URLs are becoming as ubiquitous as toll-free 800 numbers—showing up on billboards, matchbooks, and television sitcoms. The Web is a hobby. The Web is big business. The Web is a medium for personal expression, and a conduit for a commerce revolution.

It's getting better and it's getting worse.

What do I mean by that? Metcalf's Law, named after Bob Metcalf, the man who invented Ethernet, states that networks become more valuable as the number of people using them grows. A computer with an email application is worthless unless it's somehow connected to another. Add two more to the connection, and it doubles in value. Add 100 million more, and suddenly the world changes.

It's obvious how Metcalf's Law, when applied to the Web, has made significant changes in the way we live, work, and interact with one another. As a larger and larger percentage of the world's population comes online, the value of the network skyrockets. New uses of the Web emerge simply because there are so many people around. The Web gets better as it gets bigger.

What is not obvious is how the Web is straining under the load. I'm not talking about simple network architecture, although that's a significant concern for some. Rather, we need to look at how this unbelievable popularization has amplified some basic flaws in the design of our Web sites, the software we use to reach them, and business models we rely on to finance it all.

Ultimately, the solutions to many of the Web's problems are grounded in good design. I have spent the last five years making Web sites for HotWired, one of the first commercial publishers to focus its efforts exclusively online. These sites have relied on basic industry standards, have been funded through advertising, and have served a broad spectrum of technically literate users. Along the way, I've worked with some amazing designers, and have developed a few ideas on how to embrace the limitations of technology and make a site successful. Applying these ideas on a large scale quite possibly could solve some of the Web's problems.

This is a book for Web designers, but it's also a book for anyone who wants to understand the Web from the inside. What makes a good Web site? Where did the Web really come from? Why does the technology work the way it does? Am I even using it correctly?

We'll get to these questions, but first, we all will need to understand what Web design is. And to do that, we need to start at the very beginning.

Chapter One

Foundations

The Web has function, it has interactivity, it has behavior… and it is spreading like a California brushfire fanned by winds of a new networked economy.

[1]

The Web may be growing fast, but its foundation stretches back through years and decades of electronic publishing history. In this chapter, we'll look back at how the intersection of traditional publishing and early databases influenced the way the Web was built. Why is that important? Because we need to deconstruct the basic philosophy of Web design: How the integration of structure, style, and behavior form the basis of our thinking about development on the Web today. Then, from the theoretical to the concrete, we'll look at how that underlying theory applies to the technologies that make up the Web, as well as the collaboration of Web teams, and the interconnection of the people and the technologies they use. Through that lens, we can look at today's Web interfaces.

Charles Goldfarb liked to get people lost.

It was 1966. Two years out of Harvard, the young lawyer was already bored with the frustrating redundancy of preparing briefs for the firm that employed him. To burn off some energy, Charles would spend countless hours working on his hobby: organizing Boston-area sports car rallies.

As "rallymaster," he would plot courses for the roadsters on maps, then convert the courses to a detailed set of instructions. It was a game for Charles, and he enjoyed encoding logic puzzles into his crib sheets. Instead of a simple list of instructions, he would add commands like "Repeat the last six steps replacing 'right turn' with 'left turn'."

Eventually, a friend told Charles his routes were just like computer programs. "Really?" he replied. "What's a computer program?" Soon, he found that IBM would pay him a comfortable salary to write his logic-based instructions for computers, rather than driving enthusiasts. Suddenly, if you'll excuse the pun, his career took a permanent turn.

By 1969, the excitement had worn off the thrill of punch-card coding mainframes. Charles was beginning to consider heading back to the courtroom, but before he did, IBM offered him an interesting project: figure out how to apply current computer technology to the practice of law. The idea was to store legal briefs as electronic text in a database, then let lawyers query that information and

A Web Design Timeline

1965
Ted Nelson coins the term "hypertext" at the annual conference of the Association of Computing Machinery

1968
Douglas Englebart demonstrates his "Augment/NLS" hypertext system, including an early mouse prototype and video conferencing

1967
William Tunnicliffe presents to the Canadian Government Printing Office on the value of separating content of documents from presentation

recombine the results into new documents. The problem reminded Charles of the frustration he had felt years ago, sending dictated briefs over and over again to a secretary for revision and retyping—an exceptionally inefficient process.

The rudimentary text storage systems of the time were capable of storing documents and spitting them back out again—while retaining the basic formatting encoded within. But Charles found that storing the text in a database (even if that database used cardboard media) was the easy part—getting at the text and doing something interesting with it was the hard part. At first, he considered stripping all the text clean of any formatting at all, then retrieving it using simple text searching algorithms. But what if you wanted to do more compelling things than just find an occurrence of a few words? What if you wanted to get just a list of document subheads, or find all the documents written by a particular lawyer, or on a particular legal precedent?

Charles faced a dilemma. How could he store the text in a database so that it was both formatted for proper output, but also could be queried in powerful ways? A search for a solution was, in fact, a lesson in publishing history.

The History of Electronic Text

Historically, when a printed manuscript was given to a copy editor for grammatical and formatting edits, the process

1969
Charles Goldfarb, Edward Mosher, and Raymond Lorie, working at IBM, invent the Generalized Markup Lanugage as a way of editing, sharing, and reusing electronic text

1969
First packets flow across the ARPANET, a predecessor to today's Internet

1974
Bob Kahn and Vint Cerf publish a paper proposing basic Internet protocols

would include something called "markup." In the case of, say, a turn-of-the-century newspaper, an editor would scribble codes in the margins of a particular story that described how it should look. Then the codes were interpreted by a typesetter (the person who was responsible for putting together the final page on the press). Headlines, for example, would be marked with a shorthand notation describing which typographical convention to use. Thus, the editor might write something like "TR36b/c" and point to the first line of text on a page, effectively telling the typesetter to set that line as a headline in Times Roman 36 point bold and centered.

Most publications, however, defined standards for each individual part of a story and page. That way, the editor wouldn't need to write the same typographic codes again and again. Instead, each page element could simply be specified by name. Not only did this save time, but it ensured consistency across a publication. A newspaper, for example, might have defined six different headline weights to correspond to a story's position on a page. The paper's editor could save time when doing the layout by tagging a story's first line of text with a standard notation like "HEAD3." A typesetter, encountering the notation, would look up the code on a sheet listing the style standards, and format the headline accordingly. This process is known as indirection—

A Web Design Timeline (continued)

1984
Apple Macintosh computers ship, including HyperCard, a graphical hypertext system for personal computers

1987
10,000
Internet hosts

1986
SGML, drived from Goldfarb's GML, is adopted by the International Standards Organization

a concept that would eventually find its way into all aspects of publishing as well as disciplines like computer science.

Early computer word-processing applications followed a similar evolution. Much like copy editors adding formatting codes, these tools processed text with *specific markup*. The user was able to denote text with instructions that would describe how the text should be presented: whether bold, italic, big, or small.

While this may have been fairly interesting in an abstract historical context, it was ground-breaking to the handful of researchers like Charles Goldfarb in the late 1960s. They began to realize that using typographical conventions in word processors was shortsighted. Rather, they believed electronic text should be tagged with *general markup*, which would give meaning to page elements much like the markup codes traditionally shared between editors and typesetters. By separating the presentation of a document from its basic structural content, the electronic text was no longer locked into one static visual design.

Charles experimented with storing his electronic legal briefs in pieces, and labeling each piece of the brief based on what they were, rather than what they should look like. Now, instead of marking a chunk of text as being 36pt Times Roman, he could simply label it as "Title." The same could be done for every other chunk in the document:

1989
Tim Berners-Lee begins work on his
World Wide Web project

1991
First draft of Hypertext Markup
Language (HTML) released on the net

1989
100,000
Internet hosts

1991
Gopher, a distributed online repository of data,
developed at the Univeristy of Minnesota

author, date published, abstract, and so forth. When thousands of briefs had been marked up with standard tags, you could start to do some amazing things such as grouping summaries of briefs written by a particular lawyer, or collapsing a document down to a simple outline form. Then, when you were satisfied with the final brief, you could print the document by specifying a stylesheet much like editors and typographers did decades ago. Each tag was assigned a particular formatting style, and the document was produced in a physical form. Updating, redesigning, and republishing was a breeze. Charles was no longer bored. Technology and publishing had intersected in a remarkably powerful way.

Charles Goldfarb continued his work at IBM into the early 1970s with Edward Mosher and Ray Lorie. As they researched their integrated law office information systems, they developed a system of encoding information about a document's structure by using a set of tags. These tags followed the same basic philosophy of representing the meaning of individual elements, with the presentation then applied to structural elements rather than the individual words. The team started to abstract the idea. Rather than develop a standard set of tags, why not just set up the basic rules for tagging documents? Then every document could be tagged based on its own unique characteristics, but the searching, styling, and publishing of these documents could

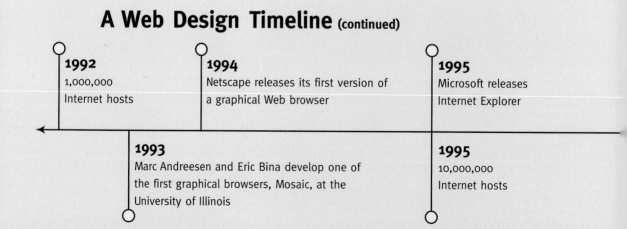

A Web Design Timeline (continued)

1992
1,000,000
Internet hosts

1994
Netscape releases its first version of
a graphical Web browser

1995
Microsoft releases
Internet Explorer

1993
Marc Andreesen and Eric Bina develop one of
the first graphical browsers, Mosaic, at the
University of Illinois

1995
10,000,000
Internet hosts

all be done with the same software, regardless of whether you were sending out legal briefs or pages of a newspaper. They dubbed their system the Generalized Markup Language, or GML (which, incidentally, also encoded the initials of the inventors for posterity).

And here's the interesting part: GML was developed so it could be shared by *all* electronic text. If there was a standard method for encoding content, the reasoning went, then any computer could read any document. The value of a system like this would grow exponentially.

The concept quickly spread from the confines of IBM. The publishing community realized that by truly standardizing the methodology of GML, publishing systems worldwide could be developed around the same core ideas. For years, researchers toiled over the best way to achieve these goals, and by the mid-1980s, the Standard Generalized Markup Language, or SGML, was finished. The resulting specification, known to the world as ISO 8879, is still in use today.

SGML successfully took the ideas incorporated into GML much further. Tags could go far beyond simple typographic formatting controls. They could be used to trigger elaborate programs that performed all sorts of advanced behaviors. For example, if the title of a book was tagged with a `<book>` tag, an SGML system could do much more than simply make the text italic. The book tag could trigger code

1996
Cascading Stylesheets (CSS)
becomes a W3C recommendation

1998
Extensible Markup Language (XML)
becomes a W3C recommendation

1997
Version 4.0 of both Navigator and Internet Explorer
include support for "Dynamic HTML" allowing
limited progression from static pages

2000
75,000,000
Internet hosts

in the publishing system to look up an ISBN number, and then create a bibliographic reference including the author, publisher, and other information. SGML could also be used to generate *compound documents*, which are electronic documents that are pulled together automatically from a number of different sources. A document no longer needed to be a collection of paragraphs, but could include references to information in a database, which could be formatted on the fly. Consider the statistics on the sports page of a newspaper; raw data flows through formatting rules to automatically generate the daily page; or imagine a catalog that always printed the current prices and inventory data from a warehouse. Electronic publishing began to come of age.

As a standard, SGML was a remarkable accomplishment. Getting thousands of companies, organizations, and institutions to agree on a systematic way of encoding electronic documents was revolutionary. The problem, however, was that in order to be universally inclusive, SGML ended up being massively complicated. So complicated, in fact, that the only real uses of the language were the largest constituents of the standards group: IBM, the Department of Defense, and other cultivators of massive electronic libraries. SGML was a long way away from the desktops of emerging personal computers at the time.

The Birth of the Web

Fast forward to 1989. A researcher named Tim Berners-Lee, working at the European Particle Physics Laboratory, made a proposal for a simple hypertext system. Hoping to connect the distributed work of physics researchers, Berners-Lee developed a prototype system for linking information including three critical pieces: a way of giving everything a uniform address, a protocol for transmitting these linked bits of information, and finally a language for encoding the information. Working with fellow researcher Mike Sendall, Berners-Lee created both a server for storing and distributing information, as well as a client application for browsing. They called this system "Worldwideweb," set it up on a

NeXT server, and began distributing the software. Popularity grew as clients, or "browsers," were developed for other computer systems. By 1994, traffic on the Web had surpassed all other forms of Internet traffic and new browsers like Mosaic and Netscape's Navigator had entered the public conscience. The Web was alive.

Part of the incredible growth of the Web has been attributed to its simplicity—especially the ease of creating documents for reading in browsers. Berners-Lee knew that a basic document format would be required for passing information back and forth between computer systems. His first effort, the HyperText Markup Language, or HTML, closely followed the basics of SGML, but with a few differences. He

Revisionist History?

Virtually any historical account is surrounded by a certain amount of controversy. Seldom are all historians in unanimous agreement as to how events actually transpired, who did what when, and what it all means. It should come as no surprise, then, that the birth of electronic publishing is equally rife with debate. Robin Cover, who maintains a repository of SGML resources on the Web at www.oasis-open.org/cover/, provides links to a number of different interpretations of what was happening in the late 1960s. He also provides the following introduction:

It appears certain to me that at least these three ideas were common already in the 1960's, often within distinct communities which rarely talked to each other: (a) the notion of separating "content and structure" encoding from *specifications for [print] processing; (b) the notion of using names for markup elements which identified text objects "descriptively" or "generically"; (c) the notion of using a (formal) grammar to model structural relationships between encoded text objects. Some of these intellectual streams eventually flowed into the standards work where they took a particular canonical shape, and some important intellectual work developed outside the standards arena. How many of the "fundamental" notions ... were (first, best) articulated within efforts that may be reckoned as belonging, genetically or otherwise, to "the beginnings of SGML" will probably remain a matter of personal interpretation rather than of public record.*

knew that for his proposal to succeed, it had to embody the following characteristics:

- **Simplicity**: Keenly aware of the incredible complexity inherent in SGML, Berners-Lee opted for a tiny subset of tags for describing a document, and didn't bother with a method for describing a document's styles.
- **Universality**: He imagined dozens, or even hundreds, of hypertext formats in the future, and smart clients that could easily negotiate and translate documents from servers across the Net. While this vision may not have become reality, the fact remains today that HTML and its derivatives can be read on virtually any computer, and on many devices like phones and hand-held units.
- **Degradability**: While maintaining a simple system, as well as one that worked across the diversity of the Internet, Berners-Lee realized that HTML would eventually have to expand. To accommodate managed growth, he added a final axiom regarding new versions: they must never break older releases of the language. So as the nascent Web evolved, it would never *require* upgrades. New versions would simply be embellishments of old versions.

Thus, the first version of HTML was created with a few basic elements: `<H1>` through `<H6>` denoted headlines and subheads, `<P>` paragraphs, `<LI>` lists, etc. Since there was no associated presentation information, any browser—running on any computer system—could interpret this basic collection of tags and display them in the most appropriate way. High-end workstations could present typographically rich documents on color monitors while simple terminal emulators could offer a stripped down version that matched the limited capacity of the device. Suddenly, everyone could exchange electronic documents, and they could do so in an incredibly simple, albeit constrained, way.

And suddenly, they did.

All Structure, No Style

So let's review this progression. Historically, editors would add formatting instructions for the typesetters, who would lay out the physical pages of a publication based on those rules. As a method of shorthand, style rules would be developed for each piece of a publication, and then editors simply would mark each section of a document with its semantic label. As publishing moved to computers, those codes were added electronically to text to describe how a computer would do the formatting. Eventually, SGML was created as a standard way of encoding this information, but it was too complicated for everyday usage. Today's World Wide Web uses a small and very simple application of SGML dubbed the Hypertext Markup Language (or HTML), which defines only a limited number of codes that any computer can present.

In the historical tradition of authoring, editing, and designing information, the Web browser became the automated typesetter for a standard set of general document codes. But you've probably already noticed two problems: HTML was only designed to encode structure—leaving the browser to interpret style, and HTML had only the most limited set of structural tags. What was needed was a way to include style rules, and a way to extend HTML to include any structural element and still maintain this universal standard.

In an ideal world, the Web would have progressed in much the same way that GML did in the research labs of the early 1970s. Software engineers, publishers, editors, and graphic designers would have collaborated on the best possible method for advancing the state of Web technology. So, once the popularity of the Web was obvious, the next few steps easily could have been achieved—HTML could have been extended in a clean way to accommodate new and different types of documents. Then a powerful style language could have been added, giving designers the typographical and layout control to which they were accustomed. Finally, HTML could have taken a back seat to allow a simple framework to emerge, letting anyone develop any set of tags deemed necessary with browsing software smart enough to discover new tag sets, understand them, and display them in appropriate ways.

Actually, this has been happening behind the scenes of the Web over the course of the last few years. The World Wide Web Consortium, or W3C, is a group of industry experts representing the many disciplines of electronic publishing and distribution. And while the Web has been moving full speed ahead into the mainstream fabric of our world's culture, this group of researchers has been plotting its technological course.

But there is tragedy to this idyllic world of the Web. As the W3C worked through the mid-1990s to build a perfect group of compatible technologies, the Web itself spread like a California brushfire fanned by winds of a new networked economy. Companies went public and quadrupled their value overnight based on the simple idea of passing HTML documents back and forth.

Look, for example, at the addition of images to the Web. Early browsers were simply text-based, and there was an immediate desire to display figures and icons inline on a page. In 1993, a debate was exploding on the fledgling HTML mailing list, and finally a college student named Marc Andreessen added `<img>` to his Mosaic browser. People objected, saying it was too limited. They wanted `<include>` or `<embed>`, which would allow you to add any sort of medium to a Web page with the much-touted content negotiation used on the client. That was too big a project, according to Marc. He needed to ship ASAP. He added `<img>` to his browser. It would be years before media would be included in a page using `<embed>` or `<applet>` or `<object>` tags; and, it would be years before the topic even would resurface again.

Andreessen packed up and headed west to the Silicon Valley, where he and a number of other talented developers created the Netscape Communications Corporation. Released in October of 1994, their software almost overnight became the most popular browser on the Web. With this popularity came a demanding audience. The Web was amazing, but it sure was limited. Why, even the simplest desktop publishing software 10 years ago allowed some typographical control. Yet Netscape's browser was limited to that simple handful of HTML tags developed by Tim Berners-Lee just a few years back. "Give us more control!" demanded the users. "Our pages are boring!"

Netscape responded, and did so quickly. Sure, the W3C was focusing research on how to best add advanced stylistic control to the Web, but that could take forever. Netscape needed to innovate immediately, and did so by introducing a set of new tags that gave their users at least a little of the power they demanded, but without the learning curve of a whole new technology.

Thus was introduced the `<FONT>` tag, and with it the capability to control the appearance of an HTML document by setting typographical attributes like the font face, size, and color. Web sites, which were now becoming vehicles for corporate communication and even electronic commerce, could now give their pages a look and feel unique from the competition. "More!" demanded Web designers. And more they got. Netscape, and newly awakened corporate rival Microsoft, began adding as many proprietary tags and technologies to their browsers as they possibly could. Almost overnight, the Web was a rich landscape of new ideas, new looks, and experimentation.

HTML continued to grow with new, powerful, and exciting tags. We got `<background>`, `<frame>`, `<font>`, and of course, `<blink>`. Microsoft parried with `<marquee>`, `<iframe>`, and `<bgsound>` and started competing for room in the specification. And all this time, the W3C furiously debated something called HTML 3, a sprawling document outlining all sorts of neat new features that nobody supported. (Remember `<banner>` and `<fig>`?) It was now 1995, and things were an absolute mess.

Something needed to give. If things kept up the way they were going, Netscape and Microsoft would eventually have two completely proprietary versions of HTML, but with no way of supporting the utopian vision of content negotiation. Instead, people would be forced to choose one browser or the other, and surf content specifically created for that platform. Content providers would have to either choose between vendors or spend more resources creating multiple versions of their pages.

There are still vestiges of this lingering on today's Web, but not the nightmare scenario that was anticipated. The HTML arm of the W3C changed course and started collecting and recording *current practice* in shipping browsers, rather than designing a future, unattainable version of the language. The consortium began a shift from *proclamation*— developing standards and handing them down from on high—to *consolidation*, providing common ground from which the industry could grow. The history of HTML is a perfect example of this transition.

Version 2.0 of the hypertext markup language was very much a statement from the W3C to the effect that, "This is how things are going to be." And, at the time, it made perfect sense. The Web didn't have nearly the reach it does now. Back then there were few Web browsers (and no commercial ones), and the users of those browsers and developers of content realized that this new medium was a moving target—things would change, and investment in content could be wasted in six months. That was fine, for a while.

Then came HTML 3. Coinciding with the explosion of the Web as a commercial force, this version attempted a massive extension of the language. While this was being undertaken, a quickly-growing company named Netscape was busily responding to its customers' demands by adding whatever it could to HTML, virtually ignoring the academic standards work that was happening at the W3C. Again, this is understandable (although very regrettable in hindsight). As a result, the HTML 3 specification never really made it pass the draft stage.

Soon, the consortium realized that unless it began to document current practices of the big commercial browser vendors, the Web would spin out of control into a world of proprietary, inoperable versions of HTML. Small, formal working groups formed (known as editorial review boards), consisting of member companies and invited experts. These groups worked to find common ground among the popular browsers, and then to extend the specification in a way everyone could agree upon. Since the groups were made up of the people who would be shipping the browsers, the speed at which the new specifications could react began to fall in line with the releases of new software. HTML 3.2 and the subsequent version 4.0 are successful examples of this strategy at work.

But can you see the shift? It was subtle, but did not go unnoticed by the true HTML purists of the day—especially those with roots reaching back into the depths of SGML. Suddenly, the simple and pure Hypertext Markup Language wasn't a markup language at all, but a collection of presentation hacks that only barely worked from browser to browser. Standardization was losing ground. But more importantly, the tags themselves were losing meaning. What did <FONT> say about the text that it was marking up? Nothing about its meaning—just some presentational clues for the browser to use when rendering.

Conceptual Model

Well, great. So the Web came from a bunch of obsessive researchers interested in creating searchable databases out of simple pages of text. What could that possibly have to do with my Web site? Can we please just get to the part about cool graphics and fonts?

Unfortunately, it's not that easy. Before we can decide *what* to do, we need to understand *why* to do it.

When I first started developing Web sites, it was for *Wired* magazine's early commercial Web venture HotWired.com. This was early in 1994, and none of us really understood much about how the new medium really worked, or what would work in the new medium, for that matter. So we looked to the traditional process that we knew: designing and developing magazines.

At the time, I was working with Barbara Kuhr, one of the founders and creative directors from *Wired* magazine. She insisted at the time, and still does, that developing a magazine was not a linear process: You simply didn't take stories from writers, pass them through editors, dump them on designers, and ship it all out to be printed. Rather, it was an iterative process. Editors and designers had to be collaborative with one another to ensure success.

"Words and pictures," she would say, "can never be separated."

Of course, she wasn't suggesting that all designers only concerned themselves with photos and illustrations—just as editors and writers are more than mere wordsmiths. The statement is a metaphor for how the interaction between content and presentation are intimately bound. It is a simplification of the intense collaboration necessary to succeed. The only way to successfully communicate through a printed page is to tie together the stories being told with how they're being presented in such a fundamental way as to achieve something greater than the sum of their parts. And when you look at the amazingly successful work archived in *Wired* magazine, you can see this theory played out in page after page of stunning work.

How then could we apply this to the Web? At first glance, it seems obvious: The Web, too, is an interplay of words and pictures—structured content and visual presentation. But it is also more than that. The Web adds a third angle to the metaphor—behavior. Web sites and Web pages are things we use and interact with in a much more participatory way than a paper magazine. A Web site can offer the ability to solve problems in such a way that we never had imagined. We can buy airline tickets or manage stock portfolios or learn JavaScript or read the morning news and check the weather forecast.

Thus developed a model for Web development: the collaboration of Words, Pictures, and Code.

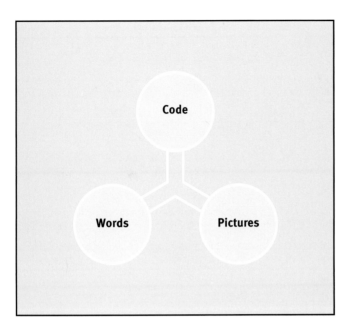

The Web, however, has its own vocabulary, and to add more detail to our conceptual model, we'll adopt it. The words, pictures, and code categories translate to the electronic publishing model with the categories of Structure, Presentation, and Behavior. So in other words, in the Web publishing world, we can extend the model to…

- **Presentation**: How that organization is presented visually to users.
- **Structure**: How something is organized and optimized for ease of use and understanding.
- **Behavior**: How those users then interact with the product and the product's resulting behavior.

As we examine the interplay between these influences, we'll see that they not only represent a conceptual model for the Web at large, but for the pages and sites we're building today, as well as for the collaborative teams that work on them.

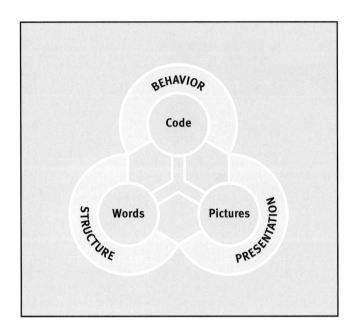

Structure

Let's start with HTML as our basis for discussing structure. We've already seen where it came from—humble beginnings in early database systems and its evolution through SGML. And we've seen why its goals of simplicity and forgiveness made it so rapidly popular. But how can something so pervasive come from something so simple?

The answer lies in the basic building block of the Web: text.

As far back as you look in the history of the Web, plain old text has been the *lingua franca*. I'm referring to the simple .txt files on your computer—like the READMEs that come with new software (also, as a matter of fact, the format of the HTML files we use to build our Web sites). But now, with all our modern applications and emphasis on graphics and visuals, isn't text outdated?

- **Text is visually limiting.** Think about it: How many stunning presentations have you witnessed? And how many of them were done by someone standing in front of a video projector showing an

ASCII-text document? Words may be the fundamental piece of communication, but visual design can't be discounted for its emotional impact. Plain text just doesn't cut it.

- **Text is not engaging.** Look beyond graphic design to multimedia—streaming audio, video, and the interactivity of other binary objects like Flash animation and Java. Text may do a fine job describing things, but at some point you are probably going to want to *show* what it is you're talking about. That's the point where you leave text behind.

- **Text is not quite universal.** Ever wonder what the acronym ASCII actually stands for? "American Standard Code for Information Interchange." That's right, our universal text format—shared by computers around the globe—is based on an *American* standard. Ever try to do Kanji in a text doc? Good luck.

So why the emphasis on text? Again, there are a few reasons:

- **Text is (sort of) universal.** As I just mentioned, ASCII may come from just one country, but the fact remains that virtually every computer system in the world is capable of understanding a .txt file in a pretty fundamental way. Some day, ASCII will be replaced with UNICODE, a system for encoding tens of thousands of international characters into text files. But for now, at least we can exchange basic documents with virtually anyone in the world.

- **Text is fast.** The bytes you find in a text document are about as stripped down as possible. Compare a text file to a heavily formatted Microsoft Word document, and the size difference will be hefty. Compare a text file to a streaming video file, and you'll start to see orders of magnitude.

- **Text is machine-readable.** This is the key. The contents of a text file can be read into a computer, and they can easily be "understood" for the words that they are. Think about spell-checking a file in a word processor. How does the computer know which words to flag? Simple pattern matching on the values of the characters it finds in the document. Compare that to the computationally intensive task of, say, recognizing the words in an audio file. You could do it, but it would be a lot harder than just zipping through a text file.

Thus, the fact that HTML is derived from plain text means that it inherits all the computer-enabled benefits of ASCII. Computers can manipulate the text. We can create programs to do all sorts of wonderful things to our content. We can index it and search it. We can translate it into other languages, and we can copy and paste it. The possibilities are, quite literally, endless.

None of these things are possible when you leave text behind. In traditional print design, for example, it is not uncommon to take text from a layout program like QuarkXPress and drop it into a graphics application like Photoshop. By turning the text into a graphic, designers can manipulate it all they want to achieve the desired effect. They can stretch and rotate and embellish until a headline or drop cap is perfect, and then import it back into their documents. But what if we do this on the Web? The words in the headline, as a graphic, lose their meaning. The computer can no longer distinguish them as words—it sees only a graphic. The machine-readable benefits of text are gone.

With a foundation of plain text, HTML takes it a step further into *structured text*. If machine readability is an admirable goal, then structure applied to simple text is the proverbial Holy Grail. Think about it: If a computer can process a file, adding structure by means of tags can provide clues to what that text actually means. For example, take the following bit of text:

```
The story was about Microsoft and Bill Gates.
```

Translating the Web with Babelfish

It can be tempting to bypass the limitations of HTML for the visually stunning impact of graphics. By imprisoning parts of your pages as graphics, you can achieve a variety of effects beyond the rather rudimentary capabilities of today's browsers. Headlines can come alive in any typeface you desire. Text can rotate and show off drop shadows, and on and on and on.

But is it really such a good idea?

For a perfectly clear example of the power of text, we can turn to the Alta Vista Search Engine. One of the interesting features the service offers is the capability to translate Web pages into other languages. Thus, if you find an interesting looking page written in Spanish (and you don't happen to *habla Español*), you can let the Babelfish translator convert it to English.

That is, if the page is actually still text. The engine can't get to the words found in graphics, so all those fancy headlines are going to stay elusive. Bummer, considering that is often the most important content on the page. And those sites that create their content as a graphic or Flash animation? Well, you're completely out of luck.

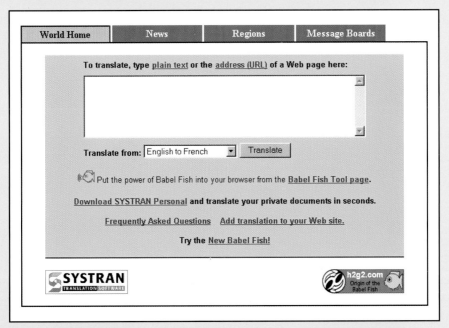

The Alta Vista translation service, Babelfish, will convert Web pages between a number of different languages... if it can read them.

What can a computer do with the line above? Well, as we've seen, it can do any number of transformations. It can be spell-checked, searched, translated, converted to capital letters, or printed in green. But consider the following:

```
<p>The story was about
<company website="http://microsoft.com"
symbol="MSFT">Microsoft</company> and
<person title="President"
employer="Microsoft">Bill Gates</person>.</p>
```

Now consider how easy it would be to programmatically manipulate the text. Not only can I do all the things we could do to the previous example, but I can add even more value. I can look up the current stock price of the company mentioned. I can build a link to the company's home page on the Web. I can link to any biographical information I may have on Mr. Gates. I can search this text, and any other text we have, and aggregate all the officers of public companies. And the list goes on and on.

We've just added a very powerful feature to our text—something called *metadata*, or information about information. The metadata in the tags is not intended to be displayed as part of the sentence but rather as embellishment and annotation of the sentence. It is adding value. It is allowing us to reference parts of our content.

These are structural tags. They talk about the semantics of a document and add metadata so that we can manipulate our content. Others, purely presentational tags, offer none of these benefits. Think for a second, about the difference between these two examples:

```
The story was about <b>Microsoft</b> and Bill Gates.
```

and

```
The story was about <company>Microsoft</company>
and Bill Gates.
```

Which is more valuable? Obviously, the second allows us far more opportunity to disambiguate the content. The `<b>` tag may render the company's name in boldface type, but it tells us nothing about the content. The `<company>` tag, on the other hand, gives us a clear idea of what is being referenced, but says nothing about how our browser should display the word. Wouldn't it be great if we could get the best of both worlds, adding rich metadata while maintaining control of the visual presentation?

Luckily, that is exactly how HTML was designed.

Style

As we discussed earlier in this chapter, HTML was never intended to address the presentation of a document. Rather, the markup language was created to merely specify what each part of a document was. And, as we've seen, it has been quite successful at that. In fact, where HTML was extended to try to encompass things like fonts and layout, it has largely been unsuccessful.

How, then, are we to do any sort of visual design on our pages and sites?

Enter Cascading Stylesheets.

"Trying to design with HTML," says my old friend Steve Mulder, "is like trying to paint a portrait with a paint roller."

And he is right. Steve wrote a book on Cascading Stylesheets (CSS) a few years back, pining for the day when we would have complete control over the visual presentation of our Web pages. Browser compatibility and vendor priorities being what they are, we've only recently seen a critical mass of users upgrading to browsers that just barely support enough CSS functionality to be useful. But the theory behind CSS is important.

CSS is a simple, yet powerful text-based standard for specifying how our content should look in browsers. While HTML excels at telling us what a document has in it, CSS steps in and tells us exactly how it should appear. I won't go into the details and syntax of how the technology actually works, see the sidebar *Getting Stylish* for a variety of resources to help you with that.

The true power of CSS lies in the power of abstraction. Put simply: keeping your content separate from its presentation is a valuable strategy. Here's how it works.

When you create an HTML document, you add tags that describe the contents of the document to the computer. By adding a stylesheet, you can also tell the browser how each tag should be rendered. You are, in effect, telling the browser to ignore the default visual appearance of each element on your page.

"Go through my document and set every paragraph in the font family Verdana. And while you're at it, make it 9-point with 16-point leading. Also, half-inch margins would be nice." And thus you start your conversation with the browser, informing the browser how you want your pages to display. This instruction, by the way, would look something like this:

```
P {font: normal 9pt/16pt Verdana; margin: .5in}
```

Getting Stylish

Cascading Stylesheets should be part of every Web designer's vocabulary. Here are a few resources that can help you with the basics.

Mulder's CSS Tutorial
Brought to you by Webmonkey, a Web developer resource, this collection of lessons will help you understand everything you need to know about CSS basics.
http://webmonkey.com/authoring/
stylesheets/

Webreview's CSS Compatibility Guide
An in-depth look at how well the browsers are doing at CSS support. Includes bugs and inconsistencies across platforms and versions, as well as a "leader board" that ranks the browsers.
http://style.webreview.com/

Cascading Stylesheet Specification
From the horse's mouth, so to speak, a collection of resources and technical specifications set out from the World Wide Web Consortium.
http://www.w3.org/Style/CSS/

Look at the shift here, though. Our presentation of the paragraph is associated with the actual paragraph by name only, not location. That means that we can change the appearance of our paragraphs—yes, all the paragraphs in our document at once—by editing one line of our stylesheet *while never touching our content*. Add the fact that our stylesheet can be linked as a separate document and linked to multiple pages across our Web sites, you can start to see the amazing change. Edit one style declaration, and you change the look and feel for an entire site.

See the connection? All of this is built on a model that dates back hundreds of years to the communication and collaboration between editors and typesetters—little style notes in the columns of copy, requesting a particular formatting. Yet we can harness this power of using text files and browsers. Our presentation and structure are both powerfully joined and valuably separate.

Behavior

The Web, though, is much more than a metaphor of words and pictures. The Web has function; it has interactivity; it has behavior.

These qualities, in fact, are what sets the Web apart from other media—from print design, or film, or even animation. In the coming chapters, we'll touch on many aspects of interactivity and behavior, and particularly how it affects design and our approach to it.

This area, in particular, is where the boundaries between the disciplines of words, pictures, and code get fuzzy. Where do we draw the line when, say, we need our pages to maintain the look and feel of a brand experience, but still function as an e-commerce application? When do designers stop worrying about color choices and page layout, and start analyzing the tasks and actions that lead to successfully purchasing of a product, or executing a stock trade, or performing a search, or downloading music?

But there are more ways in which interactivity intersects with design. Even the most basic of design decisions start to get tangled in complexity on the Web. The painfully real fact that the browsers used by your audience are varied and inconsistent will force you to develop a design strategy that includes a healthy dose of programmatic code *in your design*. The size and scope of Web sites, as well, are growing at an insane clip. The only solution has been to develop systems that generate Web pages from databases using templates. Imagine the variables: You don't know which browser *or* what content will show up in the interfaces you're trying designing.

And that's just the beginning. There is an onslaught of new technologies and innovations hurling through cyberspace every day. How can we keep up?

We probably don't have to. But we do need to know the possibilities and limitations of our new medium. And we can get help. We can collaborate.

From Code to Teams

You can tell when the interconnectivity among the words, pictures, and code of a Web site are out of balance. We've all seen Web sites only a designer could love: chocked-full of artistic touches and eye candy; or, for that matter, pages so focused on pure information retrieval that surfing them is as exciting and entertaining as waiting in line at the post office. These sites may well suit their intended audience and justify their existence, but they appear to have been created in a vacuum.

Imagine, for a moment, two Web sites with two completely opposite approaches to delivering content online. One displays an artist's portfolio through a slide-show presentation. The interface offers you a linear path through a series of full-screen photographs. The other is a vast database of, say, information on airplane parts arranged hierarchically and coded by serial number. Each site has a very specific purpose and audience. Each takes a radically different approach to the organization and presentation of information on the Web. Yet a common thread ties sites like these together.

A good Web page, of course, will be a solid blend of
presentation, structure, and interactivity. Put simply, the
ultimate goal of a successful Web site is a collaboration of
design and editorial content with interface functionality
and a solid backend system. Good design is much more
than decoration, just as well-planned architecture will take
a confusing hierarchy of data and guide an audience
through layers of information to the nuggets they need.
This tenuous balance is invisible to the user when done correctly, and painfully obvious when askew.

That's the *expression* of content on the Web. Couldn't
you use the same formula for approaching a project in the
first place? Building a team for developing a Web project is
nearly identical to building the project itself. Carefully
matching the disciplines of design, content, and programming—and managing that balance—can be as difficult as
building the end product.

Case in point: When I was working with the design team
on the first version of the HotBot search engine, we faced
unique circumstances. The group was part of a larger

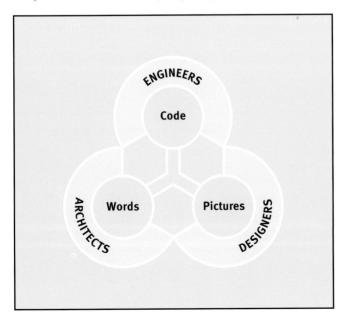

development team at Wired Digital, and we were building this Web application using licensed technology from a company called Inktomi. The problem, of course, was in collaboration. Inktomi had remarkably talented engineers, programmers, and computer scientists who had built its technology. We, on the other hand, were developing interfaces, planning a marketing campaign, and setting up a production environment. We had a series of planning meetings, thought we understood each other, then went off and built our respective chunks of the search engine. Inktomi tackled the back-end index; we focused on the front-end design. When it came time to wire them together, well, you can imagine what happened. Designers scratched their heads as engineers tried in vain to explain why our solutions would not work with their technology. Back to the proverbial drawing board, this time with much tighter communication.

The converse has been true as well. I can remember reworking countless interfaces after a designer, working in Photoshop, handed off an interface to a production manager tasked with creating the HTML representation. Without fail, the HTML guru would come back begging for changes, while the designer demanded perfection for the work of art that was the interface.

The solution, of course, is intimate collaboration between developers, designers, editors, architects, production gurus, marketing managers, the sales team, and everyone else who touches the Web site.

Right, I know, not likely. But if you use this model of structure, presentation, and behavior as a foundation for how we build our teams and manage the development process, then at least you have a head start.

Web teams are inherently interdisciplinary. Web designers may be domain experts in their corner of our triangle, but the more they can branch out—the more they can approach the behavior and structural needs of a design—the easier success will be. This communication, and ultimately translation between disciplines, is critical.

Sure, you're thinking, that's fine for the big Web site of some huge corporate interest, I just want to build my home page.

That's the point. Thinking like a development team, even if you are a team of one, is the right place to start when you're approaching a new project, no matter what the scale. Rather than just throwing together a handcrafted exhibit of art or a structured presentation of data, step back and study the endeavor from all aspects of development. How does interactivity play a role? What is the aesthetic quality of the information? What are the goals of your users, and how can you help them be successful?

You can begin thinking like a coherent development team and the choices you make will be grounded in solid answers, rather than the assumptions you had when you started.

Looking Ahead

In the coming chapters, we'll examine all three angles of the Words-Pictures-Code model. We'll see how stylistic conventions are being developed to increase the Web's ease of use. We'll look at how structural integration of large-scale Web sites is being developed and exploited. And, we'll examine the emerging discipline of dynamic design—both in interfaces and across Web sites—that encompasses behavior and interactivity.

All of this means nothing, of course, without the collaboration among those who excel at the disciplines I've introduced. This collaboration—communication, really—is without exception the most critical factor in the success of a Web project and the resulting product. Without it, you'll just be practicing.

Chapter Two

Interface Consistency

To dismiss basic contexts such as link colors, page layouts, navigation systems, and visual hierarchy as "boring" or "pedestrian" is akin to laughing at a car's steering wheel as unimaginative.

[2]

Not too long ago, it was easy to make assumptions about Web audiences.

Everyone who was using the Web back then was creating the Web as well. We

built interfaces which assumed that. However, as the Web quickly grew, the

sophisticated users became the one percentile, and designers had to stop relying

only on experimentation with interfaces, and concentrate on building sites that

were simple and consistent. Impatient users, it turned out, weren't interested in

learning new and different navigation schemes every time they happened across

a new site. This chapter explains how those contexts have developed and how

you can exploit them on your site while still maintaining an edge. Of course,

there's still a lot of experimentation going on with Web interface design, and

something called Pattern Language design will help us embrace it.

Mark Hurst calls himself an "Ease of Use Evangelist." The goal of his company, Creative Good, is to make the World Wide Web easy to use for as many people as possible (while making his clients more money, of course). By way of introduction, he offers a compelling list of hurdles the average person must negotiate simply to get started using the World Wide Web. Despite every effort of software and operating system developers, it is clearly a daunting task. According to Hurst, the path to the Internet looks something like this:

Imagine knowing nothing about computers—at all. You're standing before rows of gray boxes and monitors at the local consumer electronics superstore as an anxious sales associate hovers nearby, eager to send you home with the perfect—or at least most expensive—computer system.

So you make a choice, based on some combination of your intended uses for the contraption—probably some mix of managing your finances, educating the kids, playing some games, and, of course, accessing the Internet.

Once home, you unpack the cartons, and follow the thick instruction manual step-by-step through the installation of your new hardware. This plugs into that, this CD-ROM needs to go in first, followed by that one. Finally, by some twist of fate, you managed to get the all the combinations right, and you're greeted with a "virtual desktop" filled with icons and menus and a world of other possibilities.

But wait, says Hurst, there's more. Even though you were able to compare the features of all the systems on the market, and get your particular model home and working, you have yet to crack the operating system. There is even more to learn here—from the relatively simple task of getting a word processor installed to write letters, to the more obscure chore of configuring device drivers sufficiently to allow the eventual printing of that letter.

But let's skip over that for the moment. Our task at hand is surfing the Web.

If you thought the operating system was difficult, wait until we try to get that OS to talk to a network of other computers. It's a tenuous balance between hardware, software, and the rest of the world. On top of that, you need to do more comparison shopping, and eventually settle on a Internet Service Provider. Got that? Good. Modem dials? Great! Connection established? Fantastic.

Now on to the Web browser. Microsoft or Netscape? What's the difference? What's a URL? What's a bookmark? DNS error? 404 - File not found? What's going on? Where am I? Who exactly has my credit card number?

Ouch.

The Web is hard. Our average new computer user has just gone through a remarkably difficult experience and has somehow managed to get to the front door of your fancy Web site. Exactly how much effort do you think this poor soul is going to put into learning your particular interface?

Think about the user's experience. The experimental, cutting-edge Web design you were so proud of can quickly turn into a barrier for entry—a wall between your audience and your site.

You're not alone. Virtually every Web site is experiencing this fundamental issue: Users get confused, and many are clicking around aimlessly looking for some reason to justify their Web experience.

Web site developers are finding that if they manage their users' expectations through consistency—and not just internally, but with other similar sites—those users respond. It is interesting to look at how sites build trust with their users through consistency and how that is causing homogeneous interface solutions on the Web. Or, rather, why the entire Web is starting to look the same.

Building Trust with Consistency

The path from shopping for a computer to your Web site is a long one for consumers. One of the ways computer vendors and software developers have attempted to make this experience easier for their users is through consistency. The premise is simple: If you go through the effort of learning something once, why not use that new skill over and over again and build on that foundation, rather than relearning the same basic techniques.

The Macintosh computer, developed in the early 1980s, used this strategy to introduce computing to an entirely new audience. Every program on the Mac looked and worked the same as every other one. The "Copy" command in a word processor did the same thing as the "Copy" command in your address book application and drawing program. Interface widgets like scrollbars, close boxes, and cursors were shared by every program, both in appearance and function.

Contrast that to the first attempts at a graphical operating system by Microsoft. Early Windows programs lacked the consistent functionality assumed in Macintosh applications, and were often criticized as far more difficult to learn and use. On the Mac, every application had a File menu, and the last item on that menu was Quit, which could be accessed by simultaneously pressing the "Apple Key" and "Q." Every program worked that way; learn it once, use it over and over. This wasn't the case in the Windows OS. Quitting a program may require a "Quit" command, but might be accomplished by an "Exit" command, or "Break," "Stop," "End," or whatever the application's developer decided to use. That command could be on any menu, and could be accessed by any key combination—or possibly not have a keyboard shortcut at all. Applied to all possible commands across all possible applications, it's easy to see why Windows was considered more difficult to learn and use than the Macintosh. In fact, the last few years have seen the Windows operating system achieve a much more consistent—and therefore easier to use—approach to application design.

Computer interfaces aren't the only systems that benefit from consistency. Learn to drive a car and you've acquired the skills necessary to drive any car. There is a standard of consistency in automobile interfaces that we take for granted—the wheel in front of the driver turns counterclockwise to steer the vehicle left, the pedal on the floor can be pressed to go faster, and so on. Imagine if the 2001 Volkswagens used joysticks to steer, and a big knob on the dashboard to control speed. Lexus might counter with a trackball, followed by the Nissan retina tracking line-of-sight steering system. You get the idea....

Putting Consistency into Context

Consumers of these products aren't the only beneficiaries. The people who produce them rely on consistency, as well. Computer software developers and automobile designers know that they can build consistency into their products to avoid solving the same problems over and over. Rather than spend time reinventing scrollbars to move through a document, software developers can focus on making it easier and more efficient to write a letter using their word processor. The scrolling problem was solved long ago; they need not worry about it. Likewise, instead of literally reinventing the wheel, auto manufacturers can assume how steering works, and put more effort into more important areas of innovation—like getting better gas mileage out of their vehicles.

Assumptions like these exist in the world of print design as well, and again are seldom challenged. Think about the rules for how a magazine works—a front cover, a table of contents, page numbers, headlines, photo captions, even the number of pages and the quality of paper stock. These are all shortcuts to understanding the focus and function of a particular publication. Print-based designers can take all of these rules for granted as they develop a particular project, focusing instead on the message to be communicated.

Think of these basic rules of consistency as *context* that both consumers and producers of products can use. These contextual clues are all around us as we live our lives in our modern world. We see a red octagon while driving, we know to stop. We see a little box with an X in the corner of a program's window, and we know that we can click it to close that window. We learn the clues once, we use them over and over.

From Print to the Web

It's easy for Web designers to envy print designers. Those working in print know the rules, how to bend them, and when to break them. Designers have had over 600 years of history and tradition with powerful context developed through centuries of printed material. A magazine designer doesn't have to worry about how a magazine works. The designer can assume that readers will turn pages and, in Western society at least, read from top to bottom.

Navigation, page layout, and all the other basic pieces of a product's usability are taken for granted. *Wired* magazine, for example, broke many rules when it hit the newsstands in 1993, but the experimental design was still printed on pages that you turned from left to right. It wasn't printed on a cone that you spun on your head … it was a magazine, and despite its rebellious and experimental visual aesthetic, it still followed the basic context of a magazine.

Early on in the evolution of the Web, when the first users of the first browsers surfed the first Web sites, there was little context. The Web itself was such a dramatic step toward making the confusing Internet easier to use, that most were glad they could simply point and click. And considering the incredibly limited state of HTML at the time and the under-powered browsers that existed back then, most sites looked pretty similar anyway.

The Web has become mainstream, though, and is developing its own context. The last five years may be a hyperspeed blur of a rapidly growing new medium, but the basic context has been evolving slowly as a constant flood of new users comes online. Look at one of the most basic units in the foundation of the Web, the hypertext link, as an example of a context on the Web.

Someone once decided that in graphical browsers, links should be set apart by color and given an underline. In addition, when a user moves the cursor over the link, that cursor should indicate "clickability"—usually by changing from an arrow to a hand with a pointing finger.

The blue underlined word became one of the Web's first contextual clues to functionality. By simply attaching the appropriate code to a word or phrase, designers would trigger the browser to render a link. This would let the user know that she could navigate by clicking those words. As the technology of the Web advanced over time, allowing greater control of design elements like typography and color, the context of hypertext links evolved. Now, links need not be just blue, but can simply be a contrasting color to the text around them. In certain circumstances, such as when a large group of links have been give the spatial relationships common to navigation systems, even the underlining can be eliminated.

So context can evolve. The fact remains though that Web designers aren't required to teach every user how hypertext works. They can simply indicate a link through a well-defined contextual clue, and leave it at that. "It's a link," the color tells us, "Go ahead and click it."

While a native context like hypertext continues to evolve on the Web, we can also borrow and adapt new contextual clues from the real world. Think of the simplicity of an arrow pointing to the right. Imagine typing a URL for the fictional Blexo Corporation into your browser window, and seeing the following on a Web page:

BLEXO INDUSTRIES →

Would you have any question in your mind as to where to click, and where you would expect to go? At least in the Western world, an arrow pointing to the right means "more this way," "next," or "continue." We unconsciously assume that the arrow is relaying a message ingrained in us from years of using printed material. "Turn to the next page" it tells us. We understand without thought that the arrow will take us to Blexo's home page.

What if the arrow had been pointing up? A subtle change, yet a shattering of context, and you're left wondering just what exactly would happen if you clicked. If the

Evolving Links

Links may very well have been the first context for the Web, and it is certainly true that the basic unit of hypertext is one of the first things new users grasp. But how far can we push this fundamental understanding? The answers tell us quite a bit about how design on the Web is evolving.

It pays to reflect on where HTML started, and just how limited the presentational functionality of the Web was in the early 1990s. In the pre-Netscape era, there was virtually no control over things like typeface, color, or size. As a result, those writing early Web documents simply wrapped an ‹a› tag around text they wanted to link to some other Web reference. The text would render in blue, with an underline, and that was that.

The dawn of the ‹FONT› tag changed that. Paired with attributes like LINK and

Designer Drue Miller recommends the squint test: Squint as you look at the screen and see if the links are still distinguishable. If they are, you're safe. She also offers this example of the ‹U› tag gone horribly wrong in her presentation "Design Effective Navigation." Nothing on this page is a link. What a mess.

VISITED on the ‹BODY› element, designers could start to develop an aesthetic sensibility in their pages using color schemes. But, with any new freedom comes new responsibility. Now, a basic usability axiom could be abused. You could, for example, change the link color to something other than blue. Would users learn that *any* color could be a link? You could also, if so inclined, use the ‹FONT› tag to set

Must hypertext always be expressed with underlined text? Not necessarily. The links on the front page of the Yodlee.com service clearly point to sections such as "company," "products," and "partners" without requiring a redundant underline. Sometimes careful page layout is enough to communicate a link.

all the type on a page in blue. Add the `<U>` tag for an underline, and you could really start confusing people. And to obfuscate things even further, the Cascading Stylesheets specification brought us the `text-decoration` property, giving us the ability to turn off the underlining for links. All of these are powerful tools when placed in the hands of smart designers. But all can be used for good as well as evil. So where does that leave us now?

To this day, it is true that the default blue, underlined text will communicate to your users that the words are a link. These stylistic conventions can be changed—*carefully*—to match the aesthetics of your pages. Most Web users have learned that links can be any color, as long as that color is sufficiently distinguishable from that which is not clickable. And underlining can be eliminated, as long as you clearly communicate some other way—either through layout, or association—that the words are hyperlinks.

Just don't do the opposite: Using hypertext conventions when the text isn't a link is always bad. Underlined text will be perceived as a link, as will colored words out of context. And that will confuse your users.

It would be easy to make some sort of rule proclaiming "Link Colors Must Always Be Consistent on a Page," but there are exceptions to every rule. Here, the links into the Hotbot directory use two colors to denote categories and subcategories. Those colors match the rest of the site's color scheme and effectively communicate hierarchy.

arrow had been pointing down, however, you may have looked for scrollbars or simply assumed that clicking the arrow would move you down to where the content was. A left facing arrow, on the other hand, would probably give you the sense that you missed something. "Blexo is back there" the screen would imply, "Go back that way to see it."

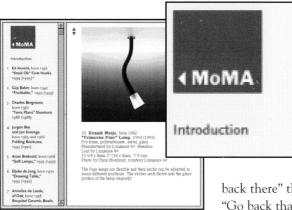

The elegantly designed Web site for the Museum of Modern Art provides very simple contextual clues. Here, a small arrow next to the logo provides a clear navigational pointer.

This process of learning is often referred to as building *mental models*— a bit of cognitive psychology jargon used by those in the Computer/Human Interaction (CHI) community. It's a useful concept that we'll put in practice to see how our Web audiences learn to use our pages.

Navigating with Models and Maps

It's no secret that the act of designing is a process of communication between audience and user. The layout of a page in a magazine tells a reader of that magazine where to look, what's important, where to start reading, and more. The same goes for the designer of, say, the knobs and buttons on a car stereo. The designer knows exactly how it works, since he was involved in the process of designing the device from the start. Since designers are privy to the inner workings of a device, or story, or Web page, it's easy for them to form a model in their minds to represent those intricacies. "The stereo can get louder or softer," thinks its designer. But without a knob, there is no way its owner would know this. By placing a knob on the device, the designer has exposed a piece of his mental model to the user through context.

The CHI community likes to talk about mental models and mental maps using the analogy of how we navigate through the streets and avenues of the cities we live in and with which we are familiar. You know where you're going, how things work, what the symbols mean, and even to avoid 5th Avenue because they're tearing it up again. You seldom get lost and rarely need more than an address and cross street to find a new restaurant or shop.

But think about the last time you visited a completely new city, especially in a foreign country. As you wandered around the city as a tourist, you probably felt a sense of disorientation, even though you still knew the basic rules. You walked on the sidewalk and not in traffic, you stopped at intersections, you understood that the numbers on the buildings represented addresses which go up in one direction and down if you go the other way. Thankfully, your previous experience with the design of cities applied to this one too. By applying your mental model of cities to this one, you made the differences that much easier to negotiate.

But back to the Web. For your design to be successful, you must match your mental model with the one the user is progressively building. Again, this is another way of adding consistency to your Web pages. Your site may have a company logo in the corner of the page. A user discovers that by clicking on it, they return to the site's home page. They've just been given a glimpse into how the system—in this case your Web site—works. If, a few pages later, the same user clicks the logo and it *doesn't* take them back to the home page, you've chipped away at the user's model. When there is a miscommunication between the designer and the user, things fall apart quickly.

What you are trying to create are a set of internal conventions across your Web site, based on external conventions from the rest of the Web. In fact, it would be useful to consider the following axioms for building and managing your users' mental models:

- External interface conventions come to your site with your users. Break these, even if you do so with internal consistency, and you'll confuse your users.
- You can extend external conventions, but you can only do this with extreme caution.
- Do something differently from everyone else only when there is a measurable benefit for doing so.
- Internal interface conventions build trust with the user. Break one, and you erode that trust.

Mental models are useful when talking about the Web. Even more useful, however, can be a specific type of model called a *mental map*. These mental maps are built by users as they move through a space. Imagine visiting Disneyland and wandering through the park without the free map they give you at the gate. It would take a lot longer to find the rides you would want to go on, and you'd probably miss quite a few. Rather, you use the printed guide to show you where you are, what is near you, and where else you can go. I probably don't have to draw too hard of an analogy to the Web at this point, we're all wandering around without one word.

Mental maps for a particular Web site can be developed almost instantly, if done with extreme simplicity and using existing models and context as a base. These are simple examples, but they are valuable in helping us understand how powerful a simple context, used with consistency, can be. It can be even more powerful to see how they *don't* work.

Broken Models and Maps

Some contextual and mental models that we take for granted on the Web may not be that appropriate after all. The scrollbar, for example, has long been a staple of windows-based functionality in graphical user interfaces. It simply denotes that there isn't enough screen real estate available to show all the information in the current document. Therefore, an interface is presented to allow the user of the document to move around the page, canvas, or window. But there is a subtle yet important difference between

applications used to create new stuff—like word processors
and image editors—and the browsers we use to find stuff.
Bruce "Tog" Tognazzini, the respected interface designer
behind the original Macintosh Finder interface, calls this
problem "hidden discoverability." He's referring to this
basic difference: When people are using the Web, they are
viewing documents they did not create, but using an interface that assumes they did. That's why, he argues, so many
people fail to understand that there is more content
extending past the bottom of the screen. They need to
scroll to see the rest, but they often don't. They don't see
the scrollbar, because they don't realize the page is so long,
because they didn't create it.

While it may be an interesting theory, Web advertisers
know this is true, and they let designers know this with
their checkbooks. Anything that doesn't show up on the
initial screen—or "above the fold" to borrow an old newspaper term—isn't nearly as valuable as the words and pictures users see first. Ad placement, then, becomes critical,
often at the expense of the user.

There are other ways that context develops and then is
broken, often by designers with the best intentions. Think
for a moment about the simple hypertext link I spoke of
earlier. As I said, it's one of the first contextual clues new
uses discover as they venture out on the Web. To them, it
means "click here to go somewhere else." But not all links
are the same.

Often, authors of exceptionally long documents will
offer a sort of table of contents at the top of the page—usually a listing of the subheads that are coming below. By
using a feature of HTML's link mechanism, authors can put
a "named anchor" around each subhead, effectively linking
to a *specific location* in a document. But, for new users, there
is no way of telling the difference. To them, they see links,
which take them somewhere else. When they click the link,
odds are they won't notice that the URL or page title hasn't
changed? Do they see that the scrollbar has moved halfway
down the page? If they've been building a mental map of

Where is the "fold?"

It's interesting to see how the subtlest of factors affect a product's design strategy. Newspapers, for example, are folded in half to fit in the vending boxes on the street. In order to sell more papers, editors would put what they felt to be the most compelling stories "above the fold" such that potential readers would be attracted while walking by. Thus, getting a story above the fold was a goal of intrepid journalists.

The same is true, in a sense, on Web pages. Editors, advertisers, product managers, and interface developers all compete to get their particular feature, banner, story, or link on the default viewing area of the browser—the Web version of the fold. The more visible a site's feature, the thinking goes, the more attention it will get from users. But where is the elusive browser "fold?"

Unfortunately, there's no definitive answer to where the browser will cut off your page. Computers can be set at many different resolutions, and users often size their browser windows differently. There are some standards you should be aware of, however. The vast majority of users have their screens set at one of the following resolutions: 640x480, 800x600, or 1024x768. By changing your monitor preferences while developing your designs, you can test your interface at those three specific resolutions and see just what your users will see.

Recent studies have shown that, as of this writing, 800x600 seems to have the highest percentage. Ideally, we should all create interfaces that scale according to a particular resolution (as discussed in Chapter Four, "Behavior"). But at the very least, check out what's actually making it above the fold.

Who is seeing what? At 640x480 (top), Yahoo doesn't even appear to have categories. Higher resolutions like 800x600 (middle), or 1024x768 (bottom) bring progressively more to the page.

the site as a hierarchy, what happens now? A link hasn't taken them deeper in the site, it just has moved them around the document. Confusion sets in.

Or consider the basic tension between site navigation and browser navigation. You land on a home page, then click on a link to enter the site. You are now one page deep into the site, based on the map you're building in your head. The page you are on has a link back to the home page—good user interface design, right? "Never leave a dead end" the old rule states. So you click the link and you're back on the home page. Your experience: You arrived at a site, you went down into it, you came back up.

Now look up in your browser's toolbar and you'll see two buttons labeled "Back" and "Forward." Clicking the back button takes you… gasp… forward to the page you dug deep into. And the forward button isn't even active. As far as the browser is concerned, you've not been back from anywhere yet. All it remembers is a long list of pages you've been to, in the order you visited them—even if you went up and down a few times. Those just count as entries in that list. So the site has a hierarchical navigation model, and it's bumping up against the browser's linear model.

Could it be possible that users, flighty and impatient as they tend to be, don't bother with mental models, maps, or a singular context as they land on your site? Maybe, in the few seconds you manage to keep them on your home page,

W3C° ARCHITECTURE **domain**

Extensible Markup Language (XML)

Working Drafts (Developer Discussion) □ Events/Pubs (translations) □ Software □ Bookmarks

The Extensible Markup Language (XML) is the universal format for structured documents and data on the Web. XML in 10 points explains XML briefly. The base specifications are XML 1.0, W3C Recommendation Feb '98, and Namespaces, Jan '99. The XML Activity Statement explains the W3C's work on this topic in more detail. For related work, see:

Nearby: XML Schema □ XML Query □ XPath, XPointer, XLink □ DOM □ RDF □ CSS XSL □ XHTML □ MathML □ SMIL □ SVG □ XML Signature

! New and Upcoming

• XML-Query Requirements, released 15 August 2000

Which links on this page point to other documents and which just navigate to other parts of the page? The links here are a confusing mix of both.

the only tools they bother to use are the ones they learned on the outside of the Web. Does that mean your Web site needs to be more like all the other ones out there? There's a chance that may just be the case.

Using Page Layout to Create Context

I loved seating charts. As a student throughout my elementary school years, I felt the system was continuously in my favor. At least with my less creative teachers, the seating chart was alphabetical—Dana Abby always sat in the front, Harold Zinser scored a back corner. I, of course, with the last name Veen, was assured a spot somewhere in the back of the class. As my early-alphabet classmates answered questions and suffered discipline, I slouched in the back of the room, passing notes and generally learning little.

My teachers did this, of course, as a way to place 30 new faces with 30 new names each year. By Halloween, names were associated with parts of the classroom, and, unfortunately, with the general behavior of those areas. My teachers would unthinkingly focus particular messages to particular parts of the room when an important point needed to be made. By Thanksgiving, my teacher would know us so well we'd be rearranged into a new chart, and for some reason I was always up front.

The arrangement of students allowed the teacher to easily make assumptions about the class, and thereby tailor the day's lessons to fit. We're seeing the same sort of "layout-based" assumptions being applied to Web pages. As a page loads, the way in which the elements of that page are arranged on the screen immediately means something to a user. Big words at the top, a vertical list of colored words down the righthand side, a text-box interface with a submit button, a cluster of paragraphs in the middle of the page—all of these things, by the very nature of their position, have immediate meaning to today's Web users. This is a critical point, because the meaning a user places on a page element may be quite different from what you, the author, designer or developer of the page, thought they meant.

And, there is a notable difference between my seating chart example and Web page layout: As users of our pages learn them and become comfortable with them, they demand they stay unchanged. Forever.

Page layout is unquestionably one of the strongest contexts used by designers. These layout-based contexts didn't happen by accident, either, but have grown and evolved along with the technology and trends of the Web itself. Understanding where they came from, how they're continuing to evolve, and why so many have adopted them can give us both a foundation for good Web design, as well as a view of a brighter future.

The Three-Panel Layout

There has been a lot of buzz around the terms "usability," "user experience," and "user friendly" in Web design circles. In a quantitative sense, increasing the usability of a Web site can be a difficult series of iterations, testing a design over and over again until every possible conflict and all embedded confusion have been eliminated. With a few simple tools, however, *qualitative* usability can be a lot easier. When we evaluate a page by asking a few simple questions, we can define a small set of heuristics that can guide us to effective interfaces. Of course, heuristic evaluation can be a complicated, time-consuming affair. But at its essence, the process can be very simple.

But what does this have to do with context? The answer is all around us on the Web today. Designers across the Web have been taking the most obvious and basic heuristics and applying them to Web pages. Many of them have found remarkably similar solutions. The result: The Web as a whole grows in consistency based on context, but innovation lags. The Web, as many complain, looks the same everywhere.

Let's look at how this happened.

As I said, the complexity of evaluating a Web site or page can fall anywhere on a continuum from very simple to quite involved. For this example, we'll take the lead from Keith Instone, Usability Engineer at Argus and Associates

and the maintainer of Usable Web (www.usableweb.com).
Instone offers a bare bones solution to heuristic evaluation.
Choose a random page on your site, ask three questions
about that page, and evaluate the answers you get. If you
are unsatisfied with *any* of your answers, something is wrong
with the page. It sounds simple, and it is. But it's remarkable how many obvious errors are introduced to a Web page
during the rounds of compromise in the development
process. The questions are:

- Where am I?
- What's here?
- Where can I go?

Try it. Surf to any page on the Web and ask these three
questions. Can you tell where you are? Can you instantly
determine what the page is about? Do you get a sense of the
overall site architecture, and where you would go next if
you continued surfing?

Again, we're not interested in defining a model for
usability on the Web right now. The important point here
is how these questions represent the most basic needs and
expectations of a Web audience traveling through cyberspace. Do they know where they are, what they've found,
and where they can go? On most large, commercial Web
sites, the answer is undoubtedly yes. But at what cost?

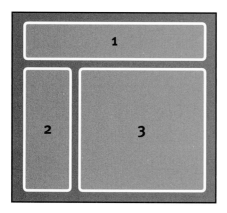

If you take our three criteria and
see how they've been applied to the
majority of Web pages, you'll see an
obvious pattern emerge.

The diagram to the left shows a
simple Web page deconstructed to
show three general regions of the page.
The strip across the top (1) answers
our first question, "Where am I?" Let's
call this the *brand bar*. A strip down
the left side of the page (2) gives tells
our users "Where can I go?"—we'll

generalize this as *navigation*. Finally the bulk of the page (3) is devoted to content, or "What's here?"—we'll refer to this as the *canvas*.

Where am I?

Users seldom follow the traffic patterns that designers intended. They often don't come through the front door of a Web site, but rather come tumbling in from all directions. Search engines, bookmarks, URLs passed from friends, links from other sites—these are just a few ways users find their way to a particular page on a given site. Localizing them—immediately telling users exactly where they are—is critical. If you've ever come up from a subway station in an unfamiliar city, you know the sensation. You immediately scan the street for everything from street signs to the direction of shadows cast by the sun in an attempt to re-orient yourself to your new surroundings. Same goes for the all-too-common effect of popping into the center of a Web site.

Localization happens in two ways—one free, one you have to build yourself. Free localization is given by the browser interface. The simple fact that the browser displays the URL and Title of every page it renders gives users at least some indication that they ended up at their expected destination. The browser might also indicate whether the current Web site is sending encrypted pages over a secure connection, how much of the page has loaded, whether the current network connection is still active or not, and a variety of other subtle clues.

But title bars, overly complex address displays, and built-in interfaces only go so far. Overt localization comes from careful page design, and almost always take the form of *branding*. No matter how simple or complex, small or big, information-based or experiential your site, the fact that it's a self-contained entity means that at some level, it has a brand—even if it's nothing more than a restating of the domain name.

Take this example: Reading a Web page, you come across a link on the phrase "Edward Tufte's *Envisioning*

Information." You click the link; the destination's branding bar immediately takes over. Did you land at a site named "Amazon - The earth's largest bookstore?" Does the site suggest it contains book reviews? Or were you directed to Tufte's own site? Regardless of where you ended up, the point is that if the site follows our heuristics, the area at the top of the page—the brand bar—told you immediately.

Edward Tufte's home page and a page selling his books on Amazon.com. How quickly can users tell the difference between these two pages? Established contexts inform them immediately.

What's here?

Users need to be immediately assured they've found what they were looking for. The Three-Panel Layout leaves the rest of the page dedicated to that task. While this may seem obvious, I'm constantly amazed at how often this simple fact gets forgotten. Designers look at their pages all day, every day, and fail to see them the way their users invariably do. That, coupled with the fact that users seldom navigate sites the way designers anticipate, leads to pages lacking a clear sense of purpose. Remember: People use bookmarks, get links via e-mail, find pages directly through search engines, and happen across a particular page in scores of other unforeseen ways.

I'm not going to spend a lot of time talking about the best way to communicate what content lives on a given page. Using clear visual hierarchy and appropriate page labels will accomplish much of that task. Simple, humanly readable URLs help too. And don't discount the power of a well-written <TITLE>.

By following an existing context, you can effectively communicate to any user coming from any direction to a given page the most basic information they need to successfully evaluate an interface. This maps the functions of localization, site structure, and content offerings to the regions of the page that users expect.

Where can I go?

I've already discussed mental models and mental maps, and how users begin to develop a representation of a particular site the instant they land on it. Our second heuristic for page layout feeds directly into this user behavior. Once your users have established their current location, they'll try to determine what else is available to them on this particular site. They do this typically by scanning the navigation that has been represented on the page.

In the Three-Panel Layout, I've drawn the navigation as a vertical stripe down the lefthand side of the page. Again, if you compare this basic context with others, like our link example before, we can draw some interesting conclusions.

For as long as there have been Web sites, there have been strategies for navigation. Even today, the Web is rid-

URLs as Navigational Context

How important is something as minor as URL structure? You'd be surprised. With the advent of commercial dynamic publishing systems, the addresses that confront most users as they click through a Web site can be appalling. Despite the fact that URLs were never intended to even be seen, most users depend on them for critical information: where a link is about to take them, or where they are in the overall site structure. Compare something as simple as...

```
http://www.site.com/computers/note-
books/lightweight/compare.html
```

to this typical example from a dynamic site:

```
http://www.site.com/computers.dll?134
5,1,,22,567,009a.html
```

In the first example, a quick glance to the browser's address bar tells users where they've landed, no matter what may be on the screen (especially when network anomalies delay page loading). With the second, there's little to help the hapless surfer.

dled with different schemes for moving users through a set of pages. From tab-based systems to horizontal labels to pull-down menu effects, there is a slew of choices for any given situation. But what we are interested in at the moment is not the best possible choice, but how to effectively *communicate* what on the page is navigation. This process of heuristic evaluation happens in an instant and occurs at a nearly subconscious level. So how can you tell a user something about the structure of your site in virtually no time and with almost no thought? Again, we fall back on context.

The classic Three-Panel Layout as embodied (and some say invented) at CNet.com. The yellow strip down the lefthand side of the page not only defines the region as navigation, but communicates the CNet brand. This example represents navigation and localization working hand in hand.

Years ago, a few Web sites—notably the commercial computing resource CNet.com—began to experiment with rigid consistency in navigation across their sites. CNet, in particular, focused on a navigation strategy that closely aligned with its brand. Since color can be so intimately associated with corporate identity (think Coca-Cola red or National Car Rental green), CNet chose a particular shade of yellow, and never wavered in its use. This color, paired with a very literal representation of the structure of its site, turned into a navigation system that stuck in users' minds. The strategy was a simple one: List the site map on every page of the site, and separate it from content with a strictly enforced band of color.

Why a vertical stripe of color on the left of the page? The decision was most likely based on the constraint of past versions of HTML and browser technology. There are very few constants in a user's environment: We have no idea how big the screen is or how wide the browser window is on that screen. But we know that the upper lefthand corner is where we start rendering. Include a background image that colors the first, say, 150 pixels differently from the rest, and you'll have a guaranteed definition of the region of the screen, no matter how wide or tall it may be.

Thus, a context was born. Users of CNet began to understand subconsciously that "yellow bar means navigation" just as quickly as new users understood "blue underlined word means hypertext link." And, of course, they brought that new knowledge with them to other Web sites.

CNet and most of its competitors have redesigned their navigation systems since those days. The rigorous consistency has remained.

Remember that navigation does more than just tell your users where they can go. Effective navigation also acts as free advertising for the rest of your site; or, to state the effect in our new jargon, a clear communication of a site's structure will help develop a user's mental model. Be careful not to judge the effectiveness of such navigational strategies based on click through and traffic patterns alone. Many parts of the page are never touched by users, but aid tremendously in helping them to understand what your site does and how that functionality is represented through its architecture.

The Sincerest Form of Flattery

Imagine the pain of having to teach users how a link works every single time you added one to your page. Your designs would be rife with explanations of how moving one's mouse to a particular point on the page and clicking the appropriate mouse button will make this page disappear and a new page from a new location begin to draw. Thankfully, we can rely on context to simplify our interfaces.

That reliance, though, can appear to be theft when applied to something like basic page layout. The screenshot below makes use of the Three-Panel Layout heuristics we've been discussing, and does so in a very effective way. Notice that the interface is labeled in Spanish. Even if you're not familiar with the language, you can discern what the regions of the page are doing: the top brands and localizes, the left column is for navigation, and content fills the rest. But this interface is virtually indistinguishable from the CNet example we've just examined earlier. When does exploiting context cross the line to simple copying?

The answer is that we need to find a balance, of course. Just as the contextual clues for hypertext have changed and evolved over the few years of its popularization, so too have those of the Three-Panel Layout. Strategies from other navigation systems have been co-opted and synthesized to unique effect. In this screenshot from an older interface from the Industry Standard's Web site (http://www.thestandard.com/), a tab-based metaphor is applied successfully to a Three-Panel Layout. The tabs allow for a sort of modal-switch in how the navigation works. This strategy slowly pushes the evolution of the existing context. Users know how tabs work. Users know how the navigation in this layout works. Add the two existing bits of

knowledge for seamless learning.

Even sites with a more avant-garde aesthetic can use the most basic context as a foundation. On the Northlight site, the Three-Panel Layout has evolved almost beyond recognition. Yet the basic assumptions—a rigid grid, a known point of origin, standard content area—again play to users' basic assumptions.

It's tempting to reject such basic conventions as an over-simplified approach to interface design. It is, after all, an exciting new medium. To think we've even scratched the surface on what is and will be possible on the

Web is naive. Yet for all the exploration and experimentation we've done to date, there have been a few strategies and design implementations that have proven successful. To dismiss basic contexts such as link colors, page layouts, navigation systems, and visual hierarchy as "boring" or "pedestrian" is akin to laughing at a car's steering wheel as unimaginative.

And we haven't even started talking about portals yet…

The LSD Design

A few years back a couple of grad students at Stanford University started a side project. It was simple enough: They began a collection of their favorite sites, and organized them in a hierarchy sorted by subject. The project grew, and the Web site they created started attracting some attention. As with most things on the Web at that time, its reputation started to spread and soon their project, now dubbed "Yet Another Hierarchically Officious Oracle"—or YAHOO—outgrew its little server on Stanford's network.

The rest of the story is, of course, the stuff of Net legend. But it's interesting to see how something as innocuous as a hierarchy has grown into one of the most used interface solutions on today's Web.

The Yahoo interface developed simply as a way to organize what was essentially a map of the entire Web. In order to provide a manageable list of subjects, a certain amount of

Using Tabs

If today's interfaces are any indication, the Web has become the world's largest filing cabinet with its various subjects displayed on millions of tiny folder tabs. Click from site to site and you'll see them. Tabs, it seems, are all the rage.

In the *Macintosh Human Interface Guidelines*, the tab-based interface widget is defined as, "... a convenient way to present information in a multi-page format. This control is distinguished by the visual appearance of folder tabs. The user selects the desired page by clicking the appropriate tab, which highlights and displays its page." You may be familiar with this rendering from preference screens or control panels. Microsoft even took the step in some of their Office applications of evolving tabs into two rows that toggle

in an almost random like fashion as you click back and forth.

But why the popularity on the Web? Whereas tabs are an effective strategy for the confined space of a dialog box, does their meaning effectively translate to large e-commerce sites? Yes and no.

If tab-based interfaces can be thought of as different views of the same information, then it should be possible to extend that meaning on the Web to different views of the same *task*. On Amazon.com, for example, the users' goal is in fairly sharp focus: They are there to buy. Tabs, then, were used early on in the Amazon interface to define *what* users could buy—an

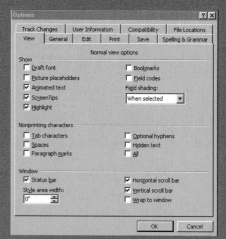

Microsoft uses a tab-based interface in Word to select modes in many dialog boxes. Unfortunately, they get carried away in some cases with tabs in multiple rows. Clicking an upper tab on the right dialog box causes the two rows to switch positions. Very confusing.

Amazon.com's tabs, while once an effective map of user goals, are now extended beyond effectiveness.

effective use of "view switching" as it were. The tabs were small, but so were the concepts: books, music, videos. As Amazon grew, so did its use of tabs. Quickly, the tab strategy scaled beyond its initial effectiveness. Whereas before, the meaning of each tab was clear, additions of things like "Auctions" started to erode that meaning. Are you to assume that clicking "Auctions" allows you to buy an auction? Of course not, but you can see how the metaphor begins to fall apart. Later, an obscure "zShops" was added, and soon after a tab labeled "Welcome," effectively muddling the interface beyond recognition.

Even worse, though, is the poor use of tabs when users' goals are less well defined. When Amazon and a handful of other e-commerce sites proved successful with their interfaces, the strategy spread across the Web in an instant. Suddenly everyone had tabs, regardless of their meaning of mapping. The definition of the tab widget began to slip into obscurity, much like overused jargon. Eventually, tabs began to mean nothing more than a random structure of a site, or worse: they simply exposed features.

Now, it's not uncommon to see a site with a tab system labeled "Home," "Free e-mail," "Search," and "Site map." How are users supposed to understand the particular meaning of an interface like this? Tabs have become nothing more than well-promoted links. Use them correctly or don't use them at all.

The online grocery delivery service Peapod misses the mark with tabs that have no conceptual relevance to one another.

ambiguity was inevitable. Thus, the 16 categories attempted to explain the full breadth of Yahoo. Soon after, subcategories were added to ease the selection process. Would you find "Recycling" under "Science" or "Society & Culture?" Tough call, until you notice the "Environment" subcategory associated with the later. The rest of the interface was an academic exercise in typography and layout. Subcategories should be smaller than their parent categories, and an ellipse would show that there were more than just the three being shown. Two columns get more above the fold. Add the requisite branding and search engine, and a new context is born: Logo, Search box, and Directory—or the LSD design.

Arts & Humanities Literature, Photography...	**News & Media** Full Coverage, Newspapers, TV...
Business & Economy Companies, Finance, Jobs...	**Recreation & Sports** Sports, Travel, Autos, Outdoors...
Computers & Internet Internet, WWW, Software, Games...	**Reference** Libraries, Dictionaries, Quotations...
Education College and University, K-12...	**Regional** Countries, Regions, US States...
Entertainment Cool Links, Movies, Humor, Music...	**Science** Animals, Astronomy, Engineering...
Government Elections, Military, Law, Taxes...	**Social Science** Archaeology, Economics, Languages...
Health Medicine, Diseases, Drugs, Fitness...	**Society & Culture** People, Environment, Religion...

Categories + Subcategories = the Yahoo Directory. This particular architecture has been copied and refined more than just about any other.

Thus, as with the Three-Panel Layout, user expectations became ingrained. The LSD design spread to sites eager to leverage the simplicity of Yahoo, and the prior knowledge users had gained there. Through 1997 and into 1999, nearly every site that attempted to compete with Yahoo (and quite a few that didn't) conjured up a version of the LSD interface.

As we saw with the Three-Panel Layout, designers can leverage users' previous experience with interfaces like this to make the mental map-building process seem nearly transparent. Looking at the Jubii screenshot, how much of the interface can you identify just by its implementation of existing context? (Assuming, of course, that you don't speak the Danish language.)

Of course, merely understanding contexts from other sites is only the first step in applying consistency to your site. You need to find solutions for *your* contexts as well. Solving design problems is, after all, a blending of external conventions and specific situations. Thankfully, there is a process for developing the best answers that goes back decades.

Users bring previous experiences with them to your site. Consider how many interface elements you can identify in this screenshot of Denmark's Jubii.com.

Designing with Patterns

As you read this, look around. Is there a door near you? How does the doorknob work? Go take a look at it. Is there a lock? What is the mechanism for locking and unlocking it? How does the knob turn? Is it round, or more of a handle? Do you need to twist it, slide it, or push it in order to open the door?

Lots of questions. You could probably think of even more if you stared at the doorknob long enough. In fact, if you spent enough time studying the process of opening and closing, locking and unlocking doors, you could become quite an expert on doorknobs.

I'm describing a particular design process in the paragraphs above. It's known as a Pattern Language, and is a fascinating approach to determining the ultimate "goodness" of a design solution. Pattern Language design has been around for some time, but the concept is generally attributed to architect Christopher Alexander, who developed the notion and applied it to not only the study of doorknobs, but doors, rooms, houses, neighborhoods, and cities.

His basic premise was that we should start from the bottom and work our way up—that is, by asking questions about very simple things, we can find the best answers and combine them into complex things.

Take the doorknob example again. Once you've become a doorknob expert, you should be able to accurately describe how that device should work. Then, you should start studying doors. Where should the knob go? What's the best way to hinge the door to a frame? What's the best size for a door? Where should it go in a room? How many doors should a room have? Now you're starting to become a room expert. You'll also become a window expert, and a floor and ceiling and wall expert. How should rooms be arranged in a house? What heuristics make for a space that feels good to be in? How do you connect those spaces? As you work from the bottom up, you'll find yourself looking at bigger and bigger issues—like how public spaces can foster community interaction, or how city design can alleviate congestion.

The process of developing pattern languages isn't confined to the world of architecture. Patterns have been developed for such far reaching disciplines as computer science and corporate organization. And, as you may have guessed by now, a Pattern Language design process also works very well when applied to Web design; even though we don't have doorknobs on the Web, their equivalents are pervasive.

So where do we start? We'll need a clear idea of just what a pattern is. In his book, *A Pattern Language: Towns, Buildings, Construction*, Alexander describes patterns as "a three-part rule, which expresses a relation between a certain context, a problem, and a solution." The problems Alexander was referring to were ones that would happen repeatedly. The solutions he proposed were abstract enough that they could be used over and over again. Let's try it with a Web design dilemma.

Starting to develop patterns is as easy as simply looking at an existing Web site and just picking something. In my real-world doorknob example, I could have started with window latches or light switches or sidewalks or park benches. The same holds true when looking for patterns in our Web sites. You may have many different types of information, or a dozen distinct tasks that your audience is trying to accomplish. But start small. Chances are that if you have a site for some time, it grew very rapidly and very organically. It may feel like the site is completely out of control. Don't get overwhelmed with the seeming complexity of your existing site. Just pick something and start there.

A simple search interface for a music portal site. This particular solution was the result of a number of design patterns derived from many contexts.

Let's look at searching as an example. If your Web site has a search engine, how does it work? Be very specific. I chose one from a Web site I worked on and pictured it above. It has a text input box, a couple of options that modify the search, and a submit button. Now here's where we start making decisions. Once I understood the technology behind the search, as well as the way my audience would be using it, I could generate the following questions:

- What is the optimal size of the text input box?
- Should the options be before the box or after?
- What sort of interface elements should the options use?
- What is the best text for the submit button?
- Should the submit button be rendered as default HTML, or should it be an image?
- Should there be line breaks between elements, or should they all be on one line?
- Should this whole interface be labeled? If so, with what?

I tried to answer these questions based on the research I've done both on my audience and the conventional wisdom for the Web in general. For example, my content will elicit a pretty specific set of queries when my audience does searches. I can look at those queries and evaluate them, which can inform the answer to my first question. For this site, most queries had multiple words in them. If, however, I had been building a stock quote server that took companies' three- or four-letter ticker symbols as input, then my box could have been significantly smaller.

I've now developed the first pattern for my language. I could state it like this:

- **Context:** Users are searching for known items by typing text into an input box.
- **Problem:** If the input box is too small, it's difficult for users to see errors they've made or edit their query. However, there are interface constraints on how big the box can be.
- **Solution:** When building a search interface, base the size of the text input box for queries on the length of your users' typical queries.

Let's continue with the questions above and see a few more examples. I've got two options for my search. The search interface is designed for a music site, so I've given my users the ability to target their query to either Artists or Albums. That way, some one searching for Rolling Stones will find the band, and can exclude references to the Bob Dylan song, "Like a Rolling Stone." So where should those options go?

I start by looking at all the possible options available to me. In this case, I'll have multiple items from which my users will choose. Looking through the form elements in HTML, I see that there are four possible interface widgets that will allow users to select from multiple items: checkboxes, radio buttons, pulldown menus, and option boxes. With this knowledge, I quickly prototyped all four possible solutions:

Prototyping all the possible solutions to the search interface problem.

Now, I'll evaluate each solution. The first won't work, since checkboxes allow users to select *both* artists and song. My database doesn't work that way, so I can't offer my users that functionality. Radio buttons, however, can only be used for choosing one selection from many choices. So this works better for this particular search application. The pull-down menu has the same effect. Users can click the menu and see the list of all choices, then select the one they want. This would be compatible with my search features, but I'm not as happy with this solution. In the tests done on user interfaces on the Web, I've seen a lot of users ignore pulldown menus. Since the options in a pulldown are not immediately visible and require the user to click and explore the options, they often go unnoticed. Of course, this doesn't mean these widgets should *never* be used—in fact, they're quite an effective use of space when a user needs to choose between many items in a known set. (For example, pulldowns work great when a user needs to select the state they live in. They know that the pulldown menu will have a list of 50 states.) Since I'm motivated to com-municate the options available, I'll choose not to hide them in a pulldown. Finally, the option list in the last example offers users the ability to see all the available search parameters, but again allows users to select multiple items. It also takes up more vertical space than I care for in this case. So option lists are rejected. The winner, then, is the radio button prototype. Another pattern added to my language:

- **Context:** A form-based interface for a search engine with multiple sources that can be queried.
- **Problem:** HTML forms offer many ways to select between different options. Which is the best?
- **Solution:** When offering a small number of distinct search options, radio buttons are the clearest and most effective solution.

That leaves us with the submit button. HTML forms give us two ways of submitting forms. The first allows me to create a simple button to be rendered by the operating system. The second allows me to create my own button as an image. Both work the same way—a user clicks the button and submits the form. Which should I use?

Again, it depends on the situation. In this case, I've factored in some of the constraints on this page. Performance is important, as is feedback for users who may not be as familiar with the Web as I'd like. For these reasons, I'll choose the HTML submit button. It has a series of benefits that make me more comfortable than simply using an image button. For example, the button will be rendered using a standard element from my user's operating system—Macintosh users will see a Macintosh button, and Windows users will see the appropriate translation into their OS. This allows me to rely on an existing external context. Users will inherently understand how the button works because they've used it before in other applications on their computers. I won't have to go through all the work of developing a "button-like" image that mimics the buttons they're used to seeing. It is also faster. The image button requires yet another connection between the Web server and my user's browser. And I also appreciate the feedback of an HTML button; it appears to push down when a user clicks it, signifying that a user has successfully submitted the form. I won't, however, be able to tailor the button to match my look and feel—especially considering that most form widgets can be clunky in the context of a well-designed identity. So another pattern emerges for my interface:

- **Context:** Submitting an HTML form.
- **Problem:** There are two ways of displaying a button on a Web page: as an HTML element, or as an image.
- **Solution:** The usability benefits of an HTML form submit button outweigh the visual flexibility of an image button.

I would continue through every question I was able to generate from my simple search interface. In fact, the process of developing patterns often leads to more problems in need of solutions. As you can see from the examples above, the particular context of my users and my content make a big difference when developing design solutions. But I also should be looking externally, as well. One effective method is the competitive analysis. With this process, we can choose one interface element, and compare all the possible solutions, find the similarities and differences, and apply them to our contexts.

Let's look at another interface convention popular in contemporary Web design: the topic path.

Finding Your Way Back Home

"Topic paths" are a navigational tool designed to help users understand where they are in a Web site, and how they can get around. This interface element provides navigation by listing sections of a Web site in a parent-child relationship, with the top-most resource at the left, and links to the right that become progressively more detailed. All portals use them, as do many content and e-commerce sites. Topic paths are a well-known convention across even the newest Web users, due largely to the fact that both the Windows operating system and the Web's URLs both force this navigation scheme on everyone.

Top: Sports: Canoe and Kayaking: Sea Kayaking: Folding Kayaks

---

A Topic path showing a user's location in a Web site hierarchically structured.

The image above is a typical example of a topic-path navigation scheme from the Open Directory Project. Note how categories get more specific. The last category, or "node," is not linked in this case and serves as the headline for this particular page.

Stylistically, topic-path strategies differ in only a few ways across the many portals and sites that implement them. Most notable are the separators used between parents and children, the location on the page, and the type of description used for the last node.

The individual children of a topic path need to be separated from one another with some sort of punctuation. That mark should have some semantic value; it needs to describe the relationship between the parents and children, or "this is in this." The majority of sites use either a colon (:), or a greater than sign (>). On some occasions, especially with sites catering to a more technologically sophisticated audience, a backslash (/) is used (mimicking the convention used in URLs). Which is best? For my audience, a backslash makes the navigation too technical. And at the font size I want to use, colons look to much like the vertical bar character (|). So a greater-than sign it is.

- **Context:** Topic path navigation of a hierarchically organized Web site.
- **Problem:** Users need to distinguish between links in the navigation system in a way that communicates the relationship between the items.

- **Solution:** Using a greater-than sign is a clear and concise way to signify a parent-child relationship for an audience that may not be technically sophisticated.

How preeminent should the topic path be? Should it be separated from the page title? Should it be separated from the page's branding? All of these questions are addressed when deciding where the navigation should fit into the page layout. Clearly, the topic paths should be near the top of the page. When a user lands on a particular spot in a large site, that user instantly tries to determine where the page fits into the bigger architecture. Branding and navigation do that work, and topic paths in particular can quickly and accurately shape a user's mental model of the site.

There seem to be as many strategies as there are sites that implement topic paths when it comes to page locations. Sometimes they appear immediately below the site's branding and logo; sometimes they take a position below the ad banner, at the "beginning of the content."

Yahoo, for example, separates the last item in the topic path and breaks the line. They increase the weight and size of the typeface as well, and change the background color to appear as a header. All of this happens above the ad banner, separating it from the rest of the content of the page. This feels artificial.

The Go portal integrates topic paths even tighter into its directory. Here, the navigation is more a feature of the page than a method for localization. The links are set under the main category into which the user has navigated. This header unit is below both the branding and the advertising.

Snap.com, on the other hand, uses topic paths as a clear starting point for the page. They begin below a well-defined advertising area (set off with a browser-chrome gray background). Once again, the topic path is being used as the definitive headline for the page. One's location is often connoted by the words that are contained in the drilldown links. Moreover, when you click on a drilldown link the topic path changes. There is a cause-and-effect that must be visible. Thus, other things equal, it is important that the topic path and the drilldown links share the same locality on the page. The Yahoo directory does it incorrectly. Snap does it better. Why put the heading at the end of the topic path? To make cause-and-effect visible, that is why. I like this solution, and test it with my users. The results are promising: during testing, all the subjects noticed the topic path in the overall page layout and could identify its use.

- **Context:** Topic path navigation of a hierarchically organized Web site.
- **Problem:** Where on the page should this type of navigation go so it has a clear relationship with the content, but also is noticeable among other page elements.
- **Solution:** If a site has a strong sense of hierarchy, design the topic path as if it were the page's headline.

Evolving Context

But where does all this leave us? We have problems to solve on our Web sites. Are we to assume that existing interfaces have happened upon all the solutions? Is our job merely to copy?

Of course not. There are as many exceptions to the existing contexts I've outlined in this chapter as there are examples. Still, there are three very important lessons to take away from our discussion of interface consistency.

- Users bring external contexts to your site. You will confuse users if you break them.
- These contexts are evolving, but the evolution is slow.
- Innovation can be found by developing patterns. Seek them out.

First, merely copying interface strategies will get you into trouble. An interface solution popularized on a successful site may work well on your site as well. It may also fail miserably. The Three-Panel Layout has its place, as does the LSD design, and a tab-based structure. There are hundreds of other approaches as well. The best way to know what people are using and, more importantly, what is working and why is to be keenly aware of the evolution of today's Web sites. Do you know who your competition is? Evaluate the dozen sites that do something similar to what you're trying to accomplish. Look at the sameness and where they diverge. Try to uncover the strengths and weaknesses of them. List as many conventions as you can, from color choice and typography to layout, architecture, and editorial tone. Only then can you start to leverage the contextual knowledge your users are bringing with them to your site. Think back to our real-world examples: You wouldn't design a bicycle with a steering wheel unless you applied only the most superficial of research into piloting vehicles.

Second, you need to understand the rules before you can break them. It's a truism that applies to everything from writing prose to riding motorcycles, and it sticks to the Web

As Yahoo gained market dominance, its competitors did whatever they could to keep up. These screenshots from 1998 show various portals' attempts to mimic Yahoo's success—exploiting the LSD interface and even using the same shade of blue.

as well. I am baffled by competent designers eschewing "traditional information architectures" or "tired old navigation schemes" when we barely even understand how people are using our sites. We're only now seeing successful strategies for rendering large information spaces. Those strategies need to evolve, but that evolution may not be happening as quickly as we like.

Finally, don't fear innovation, especially if you have a clear understanding of your audience. By using a process of uncovering design patterns (or whatever other method you are comfortable with), you can focus in on what contexts and conventions exist with your users and the other sites they visit. Solutions will fall out of a careful study of your site from the bottom up, and by thinking like your audience, you can find the best answers to these problems. It's absurd to think of a mainstream portal implementing a Shockwave-based multimedia interface to its product. It's equally absurd to picture a artist's portfolio in the LSD design. The choices you make should transcend the conventional wisdom, but only if you understand intimately what that wisdom currently is.

I hold out optimism for innovation in Web site design. I do not believe we'll be living indefinitely with a Web that mimics Yahoo and Amazon. Nor do I think a colored stripe down the lefthand side of the page is necessarily the best to communicate a site's structure and navigational potential. But how will it change? Where can we see clues for this evolution?

I find inspiration in noncommercial Web creations. These labor-of-love sites—outside the mainstream of viable e-commerce and content—are experimenting and expanding our interface vocabulary every day. Take, for example, the navigational mechanism used by designer Lance Arthur on his site at Glassdog.com. While taking its basic form from the Three-Panel Layout, he innovates by using advanced scripting techniques to create a unique effect. When scrolling the page, the block of links pointing to the rest of his site scrolls with you. Is it usable? Is it consistent with users' external contexts for site-wide navigation? Who cares. It's an inspiring look at how navigation *could* work, and a target for future evolution on any site.

Beyond simple evolution, Glassdog.com shows interface innovation with auto-scrolling navigation.

Chapter Three

Structure

Most Web sites are ever-growing, evolving collections of information and services. With so much content, so many services, and untold user tasks, who makes sense of it all?

[3]

Judging a book by its cover may result in a proverbial misunderstanding, but you certainly can learn a lot by simply looking at a printed work. Books have size and shape and page counts and paper quality. You can tell the difference between a telephone directory, a corporate annual report, and a photocopied zine just by holding them in your hands. What does a Web site have that communicates its contents and functionality? How can you tell the scope and meaning of a Web site from its interface? The process of identifying and exposing these basic qualities of a Web site is encapsulated in the discipline of Information Architecture. This chapter will give you an overview of that pure blend of art and science, and deconstruct a number of very large-scale architectures—the world of Web portals.

There are cows in Los Angeles. Lots of them. In the suburban town of Chino, some 40 miles due east of downtown LA, there exists large dairy farms that butt up against the tract homes and strip malls. These days, the farms are being rapidly chipped away by development, but in the mid-1980s, when I was in high school, there were acres and acres of them.

The cows don't all live in Southern California. Many of them live farther north, in the state's large Central Valley. Big semi trucks ship these animals back and forth every day in long metal trailers. The ride from north to south places the cows in a certain amount of intestinal stress, and after the six-hour trip the trailers are more than a little messy. I, as a 16-year-old high school student desperate for cash, had the unique job of climbing into the back of these trucks wearing rubber boots and wielding a large pressure hose. For long summer days I would do my best to remove the remnants of the preceding journey, and wonder just what my future life had in store.

Well, as it turns out, dealing with the mess of ill-conceived Web sites isn't all that much different from my earlier vocation. So many sites are thrown together quickly and without thought of users or their goals that I've begun to see dramatic similarities between them and the trailers I slogged through years ago. With a mess this bad, the task of bringing order out of the chaos can seem daunting.

Seriously though, there are a lot of folks facing similar problems with the Web sites they maintain and develop. Part of the problem with today's Web is simply finding what you're looking for. This problem grows out of an interesting force: It's a little too easy to build Web sites. Since pretty much anyone can pick up the basics of HTML, and everyone thinks they've got something to tell the world, we're left with an ocean of content to traverse and not so much as a dime store compass with which to navigate.

Fixing the Web may be well beyond our abilities, but we can certainly affect the experiences of users visiting our sites. Thinking back to the conceptual model from earlier in the book, we find ourselves on the structural corner of the words-pictures-code triangle. In the last chapter, I discussed the appropriateness of Pattern Languages in Web design, and how technologies like Cascading Stylesheets can be used to parallel that strategy.

In this chapter, I'll demonstrate how the structure of a Web site affects your users' experience. I'll start by examining a typical user experience—in this case, using a series of search engines and content sites to research a specific topic. Then we'll look at how some of the largest sites on the Web have attempted to make this kind of experience easier through the practice of integration with solid Information Architecture. Finally, we'll look at how the technological promise of XML is foretelling a future of integration across the Web.

Search and Research

How many times have you stumbled across a subject you'd like to know more about, and turned to the Web for the solution? It happens to me all the time with musicians. I'll hear something new, catch the name of the artist, then tear into the Web to find all I can about them: bio, history, influences, discography, tour dates, music samples. The Web, when used well, is a wonderful place.

Let's take the popular artist Beck as an example. What would you expect from a search engine if you simply typed his name as a query string? If you said, "Depends on the search engine," you would be exactly right. So let's start with the Open Directory at `http://www.dmoz.org`. Since this is a

A page of site reviews at the Open Directory on the artist Beck.

human-edited catalog of Web site reviews (as opposed to a raw index of sites like Alta Vista), our search for Beck turns up a fairly focused set of results within the directory itself. The most useful appears to be here:

`http://www.dmoz.org/Arts/Music/Bands_and_Artists/B/Beck/`

Here, we find a fairly comprehensive collection of sites that deal entirely with Beck, including his own official site. Not a bad start, but certainly not the encyclopedic resource I was after. I want a complete understanding of who this guy is, after all.

So off to one of my favorite music sites, the All Music Guide at `http://www.allmusic.com/`. I can spend hours here, digging through the thousands of artists all cross-referenced to each other. What this site lacks is any sort of structure—in fact, if it wasn't for the cross-referencing hyperlinks and a substantial search engine, this site may be entirely unusable. However, typing "Beck" into the search box gives me what I'm after—a pointer to a remarkable page of information on the artist. Here, I find a detailed biography, along with pointers to other artists like Beck, as well as his influences and collaborators. A discography even rates his best albums and gives track descriptions. Yet, despite the amazing amount of information here, I'm skeptical. What do the kids on the street really think of Beck? For all of the All Music Guide's depth, it lacks one key element: a connection to other Beck fans.

Off I go to Talkcity.com, a collection of community-building applications, like chat and message boards, based on a subject arrangement. Sure enough, there is a whole collection of Beck conversations happening right now. As I start to dig in, I find that *Odelay* may have been a popular album for Beck, but his true fans think *One Foot in the Grave* is his best work to date. So I head over to AudioFind.com to download MP3s from that album, and after a listen decide that I want to buy it. Now to MySimon.com to compare prices and availability across all the online music vendors, and finally to Half.com where I pick up a used copy of the album for five bucks.

This is not an uncommon user experience on the Web. I did a significant amount of research, then acted on the results and participated in a transaction. I could have had a similar experience buying a new scanner for my computer, or a new set of wheels for my mountain bike. The key to these experiences, though, is that I already knew what sites to visit to build my research to a point where I'm comfortable acting on it. What if I had been looking for the best place to go fly fishing? I don't know the first thing about fly fishing, or where to even look on the Web for information.

And that, in a nutshell, is the goal of some of the largest sites on the Web—the portals—to always be the first place someone goes to learn about something online. And those sites have largely succeeded. User tests have shown that most Web users will have a primary source of information for subjects they care about, and a secondary source for things with which they aren't as familiar. Ask a basketball fan the score to the last New York Knicks game, and he'll go to ESPN.com. Ask him the country code for dialing Estonia, and he'll likely start at Yahoo.

While most of the portals started life as simple search engines, all have evolved into more ambitious destinations. The best possible user experience, it turns out, is the worst possible business case. Think about what you want out of a search engine: ask a question, find the Web site with an answer. Two page views is ideal. This "single dip" experience, though, isn't optimized at all for companies providing Web services that generate revenue from ad banners. And the more pages viewed per user, the more ad banners they can charge for. Thus, the search engines morphed into portals. Sites like Yahoo, Lycos, Excite, and Snap began to offer services—any service—that would keep users on their sites longer. Why send users out to the external Web when we can satisfy their needs here, goes the logic.

As you can imagine, building interfaces for sites like these can be challenging at best. Not only must the designs eliminate nearly all cognitive stress from the user experience, but they must provide this experience for all possible users across all possible user goals. Traditional research methods such as task analysis and usability testing can apply in a very localized sense ("Can you find out the weather in Boston?"), but fail across the overall product.

One way to examine how these sites—and eventually how *your* site—cope with growth is to look at their architectures. For a few years now, the term Information Architecture has been growing in popularity as a way of describing how the structure of content is presented.

Information Architecture

Most, if not all, Web sites are ever-growing, evolving collections of information and services. With so much content, so many services, and untold user tasks, who keeps track of it all? In Chapter One, "Foundations," we set up a triangle of disciplines made up of Presentation, Behavior, and Structure. Presentation fell in the domain of designers, those who specialize in the aesthetic choices that enable communication and identity. Behavior, conversely, falls on engineers, programmers, and script authors. Here, we have the fundamental front-end and back-end code that facilitates interactivity. That leaves us with Structure, the domain of Information Architects.

Information Architecture is at its core a metaphor. Architects in the real world design buildings, architects on the Web design sites. How do they compare?

Information Architecture is a newly popular discipline, but its roots go back decades. Author and designer Richard Saul Wurman popularized the profession years ago in his book, *Information Architects*. This, from the introduction, does a good job of laying the groundwork for what we're talking about:

> **Information Architect** 1) the individual who organizes the patterns inherent in data, making the complex clear; 2) a person who creates the structure or map of information, which allows others to find their personal paths to knowledge.

I like this definition because it captures not only the tasks assigned to such a person, but the process and methodology wrapped up in doing them. It also sets Information Architects apart from their real-world counterparts. We're talking about data, not buildings. While the metaphor may be accurate, it's just that—a metaphor. Building architects develop blueprints for structures based on any number of constraints: the intended use, the available materials, budget, and schedule limitations. All of these issues affect the work done by Information Architects as well, but with a difference. Information Architects deal with structuring content. For example, on an e-commerce Web site, should the "Registration" process be associated with "Preferences?" Are there relevant connections between different products that can be uncovered? The Architect should know enough about how people register at e-commerce sites and what their shopping patterns are to inform these decisions.

But Information Architecture goes beyond simply structuring of data and uncovering the patterns and relationships in content. Architects also need to *present* these structures, patterns, and relationships. Bear in mind that by "presentation" I'm not just talking about the realm of style, but about how items are emphasized, hierarchical associations, and how the eye draws across the page, etc. These are all basic graphic art and design principles, but with the distinction of being specifically applied to the purpose of presenting *information*.

I prefer to add the metaphor of cartography to the mix in this definition. I think of surveyors with their spotting scopes charting new territory and carefully recording what they see. They are, in essence, evaluating a specific set of data (in this case a landscape), and applying an appropriate method of organization. They may choose a political view of the region, showing boundaries and borders that may not physically exist. They may opt for a topographic representation, detailing the rises and drops in elevation. Or, they might show the area based on landmarks, as a tourist map of a new city realistically depicts cathedrals and museums with a detailed drawing set on a simplified grid of streets.

By looking at the art of cartography, you can see the importance of creating different representations of data based on user needs. But there is another way of interpreting this metaphor: Cartography also demonstrates the need of withholding, de-emphasizing, or obscuring information in order to, as Wurman suggests, "make the pattern clear. Architecture, especially on Web sites, is not always about shuffling ten things around. Sometimes it's about emphasizing three, dropping two, and making the other five less distinct. And sometimes leading folks to "their personal paths to knowledge" takes a back seat to drawing attention to overstocked merchandise or high-priced advertisements.

Regardless of their intent, Information Architects look for patterns, then create maps or blueprints to help people reach their goals through Web interfaces.

Matchmakers

How do Web sites accomplish this? Information Architects are essentially matchmakers. Their job is to intimately understand both a site's content and an audience's goals, and then find the connections between the two.

There are a variety of ways to understand and explain a site's content, as well as the intended use by an audience. Think again about the map example above. A cartographer designs a map based on the information available, blended with how the map's owner will need to use it. A chart of the San Francisco Bay Area should be designed very differently for a airplane pilot, the captain of a commercial ocean liner, and a windsurfer. All three maps would have essentially the same information, but with radically different views. Take the same geographic region, but add different data—for example, commuting patterns based on annual income—and you'd have dramatically different results.

The same process applies to data and users on the Web. Some of the most obvious methods that can be used for organizing data include chronologically, alphabetically, geographically, or audience-specific. But this simply hints at the architectural solutions in use on the Web today. Let's look at some examples.

On his personal Web site, `www.camworld.com`, Cameron Barrett keeps an updated list of pointers and commentary on what is happening in the Web design and development industry. Since he posts these comments every day, his site is organized chronologically. Headings running down the page organize each collection of links by the date in which they were added. A calendar metaphor allows navigation through the archives of his posts, using a familiar mechanism for moving through periods of time.

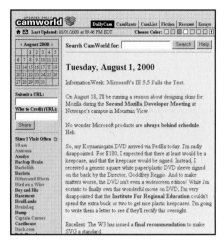

A daily journal of Web design and development links on camworld.com uses a chronological architecture.

Cameron also includes an extensive list of sites he routinely visits, a sort of bibliography that gives context to his perspective. While this list could be ranked by his preferences (best to worst), Cameron wisely chooses to list them alphabetically. In this case, since the user is being asked to make a choice from some 99 items, listing them in alphabetical order is easily the most efficient way to find a desired name.

Compare Cameron's list to the one on the EditThisPage.com site. Again, we're looking at a list of Web sites, but in this case they've been organized based on popularity as measured by traffic to the individual site. The possibilities for presentation and organization are endless; there are as many different methods of organizing a particular set of data as there are users of that data. However, the point

Same data, different view. The EditThisPage.com ranking of top-hosted sites is similar to the list of links on CamWorld.com, yet organized based on a different user need.

remains: The best solution is the one that serves the users'
needs the most effectively.

Sometimes, there may be more than one appropriate
architecture for a specific audience or collection of content. Web sites have many different segments to their

audience, with
many possible
goals. One solu-
tion to this
diversity is to
provide multiple
views at once.
Take this exam-
ple from
NetFlix.com, a
popular online
DVD rental site.
The architects at
NetFlix realize
that there are
many different

*NetFlix.com offers multiple organization schemes for their library
of movies. Each one is appropriate for a different user task.*

ways to find a movie to rent, and they built an interface
that attempts to satisfy those needs. In the left column of
navigation, in addition to a direct access search engine,
there are popup menus with a variety of organizational
schemes: by genre, by awards won, by release date, and
even by features of the disc itself.

These examples are easy. All of these sites have simple
architectures based on well-defined user tasks. The
CamWorld Web site provides a snapshot of the happenings
in the Web design industry, while EditThisPage.com offers a
way to find the most popular of its hosted sites. NetFlix
allows users to find a movie by genre, actor, or even mood—
a good example of offering alternative organizational systems to a single set of information.

Some sites, however, don't have the luxury of well-
defined methods of organization. Software publisher Adobe
Inc. is a good example. While they certainly have a strong

grasp on the goal of their site—to provide inspiration and support for the users of their digital publishing tools—the method they use in organizing their content is an excellent case study in developing user-centered architecture.

The creators of the Adobe Web site realized that the various members of its audience would have a variety of tasks to accomplish. Some may be interested in purchasing software. Others may need technical help with one of their tools. Still others may simply be looking for ideas to incorporate into their work. To satisfy these goals, Adobe offers a few different entry points to the library of information on their site. The home page, for example, offers flashy teasers into high-profile content, ostensibly with the dual goals of selling software and inspiring existing owners. The site really shines, however, when a user needs a specific bit of information. Using classic techniques from the information sciences, Adobe offers three methods for digging into their content repository: search, site map, and index.

The search engine works as you would expect. Type a query, get a list of possible matches from a full text index of the site. The site index works much like an index in a book would. Individual topics are carefully selected from the pages of the site, then given descriptive titles and organized in an alphabetical list. Compare the index page with the site map, which takes broad topic areas—in this case Adobe's products—and presents a conceptual overview of the entire site.

Finding stuff on Adobe's site becomes a matter of deciding just what method of organization you find the most appropriate to the task at hand. Think of the different tasks associated with, say, getting information on Photoshop's Gaussian Blur filter. "Simple," I might think. "I'll just create a page on that filter in the site's Photoshop area." But remember, Information Architecture is not only the discipline of organizing information, but getting people to that information. And I'd need to be keenly aware of *why* people would want information on that particular filter. A site index may lead my users directly from the "G" section to

Adobe uses different methods for organizing the content across their Web site. All three interfaces provide access to the same pages on the site, but with different user goals in mind. Shown are Adobe's search engine (top), product-based site map (middle), and alphabetical resource index (bottom).

the page on that filter, but won't allow them to find other filters that do similar blurring effects. Nor will that architecture show which other Adobe products use the same Gaussian blur filter. (In fact, almost all of them do.) And none of these systems point to last week's press release on the third-party company partnering with Adobe to do a suite of new filters.

Each view has a significantly different perspective on both the available content and the reason that content would be valuable to a specific group of users. In fact, audience-specific architectures can be the simplest form of organizing content or features of a Web site. Look, for example, at the interface on Guru.com. This site has content that serves two very specific groups of people—independent professionals, and the people looking to hire them. The site has been organized cleanly down these lines and even bases its identity on the division. The front page is divided into two distinctly colored areas—one for each audience group. After following a link on one side or the other, the resulting interface design maintains your "color choice," essentially reaffirming the architecture through presentation.

But as sites grow larger and more complex, how can they accommodate the infinite user tasks and still provide a consistent mental model? Many sites typically rely on taxonomy and hierarchy to communicate the overall structure of their offerings to users, helping them feel as comfortable as possible with their virtual surroundings. Taxonomy is a bit of librarian jargon for how things are classified. Think of the Dewey Decimal System or the subject categories in the Library of Congress. Both are vast naming schemes for information spaces. Taxonomies help us understand the world around us by labeling the things with which we need to interact. A Web site is no exception. The basic architecture of a site starts with a taxonomical foundation.

There are many ways in which they accomplish this. Let's look at three from some of the largest and most complex sites on the Web.

Guru.com offers a clean distinction between the two audience groups its research identified: independent professionals and those who hire them.

Taxonomy vs. Hierarchy

Discussions and debates of Information Architecture will undoubtedly lead to the use of the terms "taxonomy" and "hierarchy." Both of these words hold an undeniable place in the cannon of the discipline, but all too often they are used interchangeably, and therefore incorrectly.

To be clear, taxonomy refers to classification systems—typically scientific naming schemes for things like plants, animals, chemicals, elements, etc. Information Architects use this term to refer to the labeling systems and nomenclature of things like the sections of a Web site, or the various product groups in an e-commerce system.

Hierarchy, on the other hand, references a top down organizational structure—imagine your family tree or a corporate org chart. Hierarchical relationships are typical fairly rigid parent/child systems, and are often valuable for browsing large amounts of subject-based information.

Not all taxonomies, therefore, are hierarchical. The names of weekdays, for example, are a taxonomy of sorts—Monday, Tuesday, Wednesday, etc.—but they aren't organized in a top-down structure; they are sequential. Likewise a train schedule may have a taxonomy of route names, but is organized chronologically.

The Matrix

Yahoo's original interface had one goal: Help users find Web sites. Thus, it helped defined the look and feel of search engines by providing two key elements, a search interface for direct input of queries, and a browse interface for disambiguation and category hunting. While this certainly satisfied many users' goals on some level, it failed to provide Yahoo with a substantial business model. Thus the interface evolved into what it is today: The same basic user goals surrounded by and peppered with snares designed to keep the audience within the confines of the portal. Stock quotes, free e-mail, sports scores, etc., all combined to entice folks to come to the site, stay as long as possible, and come back often.

To execute quickly, most portals—Yahoo included— began to *license* content rather than create it themselves. Rather than spend time and money becoming experts at, say, financial news, why not just sign a deal with CBS Marketwatch and add the services as quickly as possible? Portals were quickly able to spread their reach across numerous vertical content areas.

Services, however, were another story. Free e-mail, or calendaring, or online address books were guaranteed "sticky" services that resulted in repeat visits and numerous page views—perfect for getting more page views of the audience they were reaching with the newly licensed content. However, these services, once built, only required a minimum level of maintenance. This marked a dramatic cost difference from content services, which required large, talented, and expensive staffing. The portals responded by buying the services, or even developing them in-house. The suite of content and services began to feel complete.

But there was a problem. The last thing the portals wanted was a "single dip" user experience in which users come for one reason, fulfill a goal, and leave. Rather, a well-designed site would *integrate* as much content and as many services as possible, providing as many opportunities to cross-sell its offerings as possible.

So let's map out this structure, which I'll call The Matrix (because I absolutely loved the movie, but in a bigger sense because it is an accurate description of what's going on here...). The Matrix is made up of the vertical content areas bisected by horizontal services. Each intersection is a point of possible integration. The more points that a portal can execute, the more complete their service will be perceived by users. It's a network effect—the more destinations you have on your site, the more opportunities you have to make connections between those destinations. And more connections mean a more complete user experience, and therefore more value for any particular user. And, of course, the more value you give to the user, the stronger the relationship you can build with them. More relationships, more traffic, more revenue—everybody is happy!

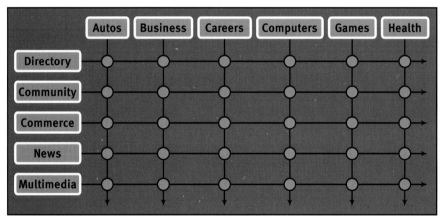

Horizontal services intersect vertical content areas to create the "Matrix" architecture used by major portal sites like Yahoo, Go, and Snap.

The chart above illustrates the overall Matrix architecture. Looking down the left column, we find services that touch all of the content areas. Each portal, for example, has a subject-based directory of Web site reviews. You can usually find these on the site's home page rendered as a alphabetical list of categories, typically underscored with subcategories. (And, they're almost all the same—"Arts &

Entertainment," "Business & Economy," "Computers & Internet," etc.) These directories are almost always organized hierarchically; as a user clicks from page to page, they move deeper into more specific subjects. Thus, the front doors are simply showing the top level of a categorical tree of subjects. You can see these categories on the chart in the first row across the top.

Under Directory in the Matrix is Community. I'm using this term to refer to Web applications that allow users to participate either by using chat rooms, message boards, or other interactive features. These areas are popular with portals because of the "stickiness" they create—an awful industry jargon for features which attract users to a site and keep them there—conjuring images of a Roach Motel or flypaper. Regardless, these features can also be categorized hierarchically. People chat or post messages about subjects, and these subjects can be matched to the ones we just looked at in the Directory. Those same subjects can be cross-referenced to appropriate news headlines aggregated from a variety of sources. And there always seems to be room for e-commerce in sites like this; a catalog of potential products can map to those same subject areas. We can start to see a model for integration.

In aggregate, these services could ostensibly create a simple yet robust architecture. But that assumes a lot. Will an architecture like this scale with a growing site? Will users understand it? Is hierarchy even the appropriate foundation?

Hierarchies seem to come naturally to portals. While debate continues as to the ultimate effectiveness of a top-down Information Architecture, this strategy has proven best of the worst, as it were. As we look at the horizontal services, or methods for organizing information and explaining that to users, we can see multiple hierarchies at work. Each portal has a directory of Web site reviews. Each portal has community space for users to interact with one another—also sorted by category. Each portal has had to respond to the pressures of generating revenue by adding e-commerce functionality to its site, and the products available for sale also form a hierarchy. With so many hierarchies, how can these sites explain the sheer quantity of stuff available, let alone add a layer of understanding to it all?

Yahoo's Impulse Buying

Each portal that we'll look at has its own method of exposing The Matrix. Yahoo, for example, uses what I'll call the "Impulse Buy" method. Yahoo.com is massive in both its breadth and depth. They've been successful at responding to nearly every trend that has blown through the Web, be it

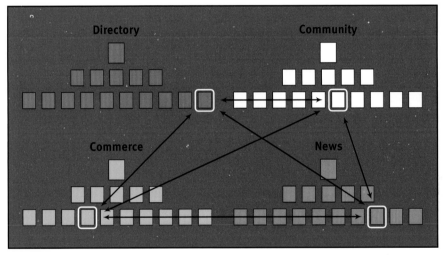

The "Impulse Buy" architecture takes multiple hierarchies and integrates them case by case, one opportunity at a time.

virtual greeting cards, fantasy sports leagues, or content for kids. What Yahoo has also excelled at has been its ability to integrate disparate content and services. As we've seen in our Matrix, each intersection of horizontal services with vertical content is an opportunity, and by examining Yahoo's integration strategy, we can see them taking full advantage of this.

In this screenshot from Yahoo's sports vertical, we can see a number of successful integration points. Each one, you'll notice, is targeted specifically at an assumed user task

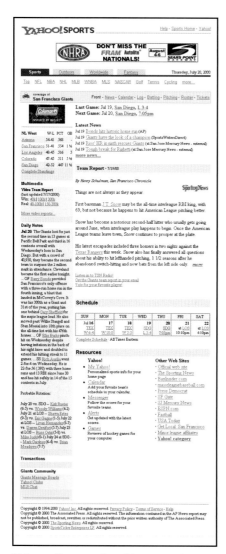

Yahoo offers a suite of integrated services from nearly every page. Here, a report on a baseball team also points to an online calendar, community services, a directory of Web sites, and more—all contextually.

at a specific moment in the user experience. Just as you'll see bottles of Caesar Dressing by the Romaine lettuce in the supermarket, links to "San Francisco Giants Message Boards" are linked prominently. This connection is obvious. But think of the scale here. Yahoo has countless pages across thousands of subjects. The size of its Matrix is phenomenal. Plus, we're not just talking about one to one links. This Sports page, for example, also links to its online calendar application by giving readers the ability to add the Giants' games to their daily schedule. There are links into the appropriate places in Yahoo's directory. And yet they are able to manage the integration in every place that makes sense across its gigantic site.

What Yahoo sacrifices, though, is an overall structure. Look at its home page. Sure, the directory of mini-reviews appears well structured. It's a cohesive grouping of categorical links, all arranged alphabetically. But this is a *subject*-based taxonomy, not a *task*-based integration. The tasks, along with content features, and other services are merely listed across the top, and are ordered, I'm guessing, by either user popularity or by revenue-generating capacity. Regardless, it's not a system that quickly communicates what the heck this Yahoo thing is. It's not surprising that new users, when asked to describe the service, call it, "A search engine with... uh... other stuff too."

Would it be possible to offer this level of task and subject integration and still give users a sense of how it all fits together? It's a daunting task, but some have tried.

Snap's "Uber-Tree"

Snap.com takes a different approach. Snap is one thing and one thing alone: a hierarchy. Everything on the site fits in to this Uber-Tree in some way, no matter what. The portal is aggressive and rigorous in its organization. Whereas Yahoo had offered links between relevant chunks of the site, Snap mushes them all together. Clicking through into the "Health" branch of the hierarchy, we're presented with a list of subcategories to further disambiguate what we're

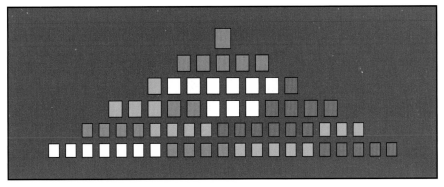

Snap merges everything—absolutely everything—into one grand hierarchical structure... whether it fits or not

after. So far, the experience is identical to every other directory on the Web. We have the topic path navigation, the columns of links ... but then things start to look a little less familiar. Rather than the obligatory collection of Web site reviews, we're instead offered links into targeted Lifestyle content. Feature stories are followed by news headlines and e-commerce opportunities, as well as peeks into the offerings of "premier partners." Only then do we see pointers to the external Web. Snap has effectively integrated a slew of content and services together into a seamless whole.

So why is Snap successful at bringing this integration together while Yahoo isn't? Part of the reason probably stems from Snap's original strategy, which was to bluntly copy Yahoo a number of years ago. Since Snap could start from scratch, they were able to apply a much more prominent structure to their growth than Yahoo.

Yet, despite all the benefits of consistency and structure, Snap often suffers under its own rigor. Navigating through the site, you'll find loops and weird "diagonal" navigation shifts as the taxonomists at Snap attempt to shoehorn another feature or service into their pre-imposed tree. One of the most important axioms in the discipline of Information Architecture states that designers are the ones who uncover patterns inherent in data, and expose them in an interface. Snap, on the other hand, does exactly the opposite: applying data to pre-existing and artificial patterns.

Go's Stackonomy

Finally, Go.com attempts to blend both of these strategies. Their interface incorporates countless Impulse Buys with a rigorous structure. They even go a step further, attempting

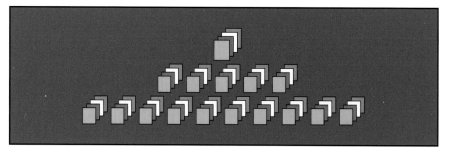

Go attempts to line up their multiple taxonomies, but finds too many holes.

to create an interface to explain it all to its audience. Unlike Snap, which relies on the conventions of a directory to expose structure, or Yahoo which doesn't bother, Go uses a tab-based interface metaphor to expose an interesting "Stack of Taxonomies"—or *Stackonomy*—structure. Here, multiple hierarchies are laid on top of one another, with connections attempted where they match.

At the top level, we're given a fairly standard portal interface: a search box perched above a directory. But between the two, tabs denote a sense of the scope of Go.com's site. We've entered the portal through the "Home" tab, but we can also access the "Community" area, as well as the obligatory "Shopping" link and a "Search" tab. Go.com is attempting to tell us just how much stuff they've got, and exactly how it's organized. Think of the portal as a cube, with different views of its content on each face—clicking a tab is like spinning the cube around. But enough with the mixed metaphors.

Drill down into Sports, and we see Sports content; click on Baseball and the content gets more specific. Here's the really interesting part: Now that we've drilled down into Baseball, the tabs across the top of the page now take us to contextually relevant parts of the site. Thus, the Community tab now points to chat rooms and message boards pertaining to—that's right—Baseball. The Commerce tab offers memorabilia and souvenirs for your favorite team, Search offers a Web site directory. Could this be the ultimate in integration we've been searching for? Might we be looking at a true representation of The Matrix?

Unfortunately, no. While Go.com is certainly on the right theoretical track, they fail to really pull it off. Our baseball example is a good one; but it is, I'm afraid, a rare example where Go actually has relevant content in all the horizontal services. In most cases, users are unceremoniously dumped "up" a few levels in the hierarchy when the appropriate content for that subcategory isn't available. Click down on the Computers link, and follow it down into Software, then Utilities, then Fonts. You should assume that all the tabs on this page are somehow related to Typography in some way. You should, but you'd be disappointed. There are no message boards on Fonts or

Typography, so clicking the Communities tab sends you diagonally to boards discussing Computers. The Commerce tab merely links you to Software in general. And on and on throughout Go.com—the intent is there, but the execution is lacking.

And the winner is...

Has anybody done it right? Not yet. While Go makes the most ambitious attempt at explaining the level of integration, they also have failed at executing. Conversely, Yahoo has done an excellent job of integrating its various services, but never actually communicates the overall integration structure to their audience.

Just as a good classification system will spawn prediction in information retrieval, a good integration structure will do the same with services. If a user can imagine how pieces of the puzzle will fit together, they will seek out integration that they assume exists. This is an excellent way of building a strong relationship between a user's goals and a site's offerings, and therefore increasing the level of trust your users commit to you. And that's good.

Taking the best practices from all three strategies will ultimately be the answer: Smart integration at a user's decision-making point, coupled with a strong sense of hierarchy, communicated by exposing a simple, overall structure.

These sites are trying—with various levels of success—to shape and order the chaotic world of the Net. But they can ultimately never hold back the avalanche of information constantly tumbling down the slopes of the Web. Why? Look for the answer where it always seems to be: Follow the money.

Yahoo, Lycos, Go, and all the others share a common trait—they are all trying to provide a *proprietary experience* on top of a *free resource*. It's an admirable goal, but one destined to come up short as soon as money starts to change hands. See, in order for a deep structure to be exposed in a consistent interface, there needs to be content available. This is architecture, after all. We need raw materials to create our building once the blueprints have been drawn. So to get content, these

Web portals do deals with folks who actually have stuff: Yahoo republishes Reuters news feeds; Go points to ESPN for sports scores and statistics. And as we've seen, they try to stitch it all together with different structural strategies.

But even if you could fill the entire portal structure with content you still wouldn't create a product that satisfied the goal. You would simply have one partner for each content area, and you'd have effectively and seamlessly integrated them all together. But what about the rest of the Web? What about the hundreds of millions of other content sources mingling out in the real world?

But, as we've seen when deconstructing the architecture of the leading portals, there's no way for them to keep up. No one site can give me as deep an experience of researching Beck that I described above. Nor can one site ever hope to offer the breadth of subjects and services that would allow me to find any information on any subject and let me act on it with as many possible choices.

A global repository of human knowledge may be a admirable goal and the large commercial portal sites may valiantly struggle to achieve this, but few of us are working on such a scale. For most Web sites, simple integration can play a role in providing a complete and compelling user experience.

For example, my marathon-obsessed wife recently pointed out a frustration with an e-commerce site offering running shoes for sale. The site had an extensive selection of shoes and good prices, but more importantly, had a well maintained and vibrant message board system used by fellow runners. The site was rich in first-hand reports from different levels of runners on what shoes worked for what types of feet, running styles, and terrain. Yet, surprisingly, the individual message boards were not linked to the individual shoes. In fact, a potential buyer of a pair of Nikes was offered no indication that there were dozens of postings in the message boards about those exact shoes. Similarly, a user who happened to stumble across the community area of the site wouldn't see an offer to buy the shoes being discussed. An obvious opportunity of integration squandered.

RoadRunnerShoes.com may have an incredible selection of gear for runners, but the site misses a key integration opportunity. On the left, a page offers a pair of shoes for sale. On the right, a lengthy page of postings from actual runners about the merits of these shoes. Yet the site offers no link between the two.

Remember, architecture must meet user needs.

The running shoe site is a good example of The Matrix at a much smaller scale. In fact, the theoretical Matrix I've been talking about can be used as an actual tool for accomplishing the integration between message boards and products for sale in this scenario. Imagine an Excel spreadsheet with services across the top row of cells: Product, Message board, Professional Review, etc., and a column of model numbers from the shoes running down the left side. The seemingly daunting task of integration becomes a matter of filling in the intersecting cells of the spreadsheets with URLs. For example, the intersection of "Asics Gel Kayano" and "Message boards" would be a specific address. As would the point where "Brooks Radius 257" and "Professional Review" intersects. The site architect would then fill in the rest of the spreadsheet with the resulting connections, and then get to work adding the links to every page—that is, if he or she was doing this by hand. The spreadsheet in this example could very well be a table in a database that was used to automatically generate the correct links on the correct pages. We'll talk more about this kind of dynamic content management in Chapter Eight, "Object-Oriented Publishing."

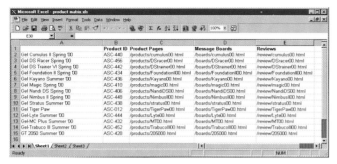

A hypothetical example of using an Excel spreadsheet to record and manage integration of products, services, and content on an e-commerce Web site.

Extending the Web

Of course, it would be a lot easier to manage content integration and architectures like the one I've described if content was richer. In the first chapter, I described the difference between presentational tags like <FONT> and purely structural tags like, say, <COMPANY>. I showed how, when rich semantic information is added to content, it becomes a lot easier to manipulate that content and add interesting features.

The Extensible Markup Language (XML) works this way. Developed by the W3C, XML takes some of the rules of HTML and generalizes them. Rules like surrounding elements with angle brackets (< >) and ending tags with a backward slash (/) have been compiled and standardized. What this means is that now anyone can create a set of tags, and anyone else can use them with relative ease.

Lots of people have been creating their own collections of tags for a while now. Markup languages created as XML vocabularies have proliferated for things as diverse as shipping invoices to musical notation to voicemail applications. And once a group has agreed on a set of common tags, sharing data becomes so much easier. In the past, this sort of data exchange was a daunting task. Say, for example, a manufacturer wanted to be able to track inventory with one of its partners. The two companies would have to agree on a format of the data, how to check if it was valid, how to

Schema Repository

With so many different types of data from so many different groups, how can we possibly keep track of them all? One proposal has been to create a repository of schemas—in essence a library catalog of all the standard vocabularies in the world. The idea is simple: As industry organizations and standards bodies decide on a common format for, say, newspaper advertising or music notation, the resulting schema would be placed in a repository and given a unique address. That way, if I use a certain vocabulary in a document, I can simply include a link to the appropriate schema. When you visit my page, your browser can follow the link, see how the XML is structured, and do what it needs to do—all on its own.

And, as is almost always the case when something this big is at stake, there are two groups developing schema vocabularies—a sort of open source industry consortium under the guise of XML.org, and an alternative commercial version spearheaded by none other than Microsoft at biztalk.org.

But where schemas ultimately live isn't nearly as interesting as what they can ultimately do. As we've seen in this chapter, global repositories of data structures aren't just exciting for librarians and scientists, but can radically change the way we think about our own Web sites.

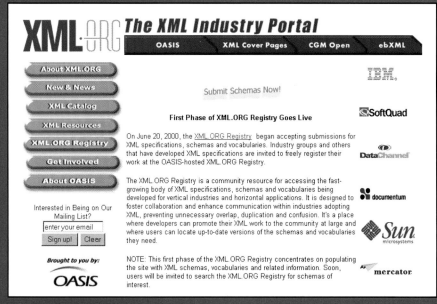

One of the schema repositories being developed on the Web. XML.org hosts hundreds of different XML vocabularies for describing everything from musical notation to molecular compounds.

read and write that data, how send the data back and forth in a secure way, and on and on. Now, with XML, the two parties can simply agree on a set of tags. Web servers, freely available XML parsers, and lots of other common pieces of infrastructure are already in place.

With this in mind, let's look again at our running shoe Web site example. One way the company could add value to the e-commerce experience of its customers would be to include reviews from some professional editorial source. But again, keeping track of the relationships between all of that content could easily scale out of control—especially considering the other points of integration that are possible.

The running shoes could be organized with an XML vocabulary—or "schema" as they're commonly called—that would look something like this:

```
<product>
  <id>401K8-H</id>
  <manufacturer>Asics</manufacturer>
  <name>Kayano Gel</name>
  <price type="retail" currency="US">89.95</price>
</product>
```

The company could have one, simple, text document for each product, stored on a Web server with a unique URL. As could any potential partner. A magazine with reviews of running shoes, for example, could have a similar collection of XML documents, each formatted something like this:

```
<content type="review">
  <headline>Getting the Lead Out</headline>
  <subhead>Asics speeds up it's line for 2000</subhead>
  <date format="dd/mm/yyyy">11/16/1999</date>
  <author>Sarah Conner</author>
  <product>Asics Kayano Gel</product>
  <para>It wasn't long ago that I first noticed a change
    in the way Asics shoes felt…</para>
</content>
```

Now, with well structured and described content, both companies will have a much easier time integrating with each other. With each offering content based on well-defined industry standards, the process would be straightforward. The shoe company can download a free, open source software tool called a parser, which is designed specifically for XML data. It will work with its Web server, and whatever standard scripting languages the engineers are comfortable with. And they will write a simple script that will search through the magazine's XML looking for each instance of a "product" tag contained within a "content" tag that is of type "review". When it finds a match, this script will build a link on the appropriate page. Maybe the e-commerce site's architect will suggest this be displayed with a tab-based interface like Go.com's Stackonomy. Maybe they'll use a Uber-Tree like Snap.

If you have much experience with building Web sites, you may be thinking, "Well, sure they could do that. But we've always been able to do that with databases or even comma-separated text files!" And you'd be right. But the point of XML is not that it opens uncharted technological capabilities. Rather, the promise of XML is much like the promise of HTML—it makes something that was fairly challenging and complicated much, much easier. Before XML, engineers would have to decide on a data format, how to check for validity of that data, a communication protocol, a security mechanism, and much more. Now, they can simply trade schemas and get back to work.

Early on in the development of the Web, it became clear that HTML—despite all of its limitations—solved a very real problem. With a few simple tags, it was suddenly possible to distribute content to anyone with a connection to the network in a standard way. The seemingly impenetrable maze of the Internet gained a consistency that paved the way for a whole new economy.

Now, with XML, the same starts to become true for *all* data. In the very near future, we may forget entirely about arcane file formats for things like our address book, e-mail applications, word processors, and spreadsheets. Businesses may stop worrying about integrating their inventory systems with their shipping schedules and suppliers. And Web sites will find it easier and easier to offer the full services their audience expects.

Fitting It Together

I hope you'll take away from this discussion a sense of how important structure really is. Information Architecture is only one leg in our overall model of Structure, Presentation and Behavior, but it's dramatic in how it connects us. It encompasses not only the most basic organization of a Web site, but the integration of your content. And it has as much to do with Web design as pixels, colors, and typography.

Chapter Four

Behavior

Much like a print designer's knowledge of inks on paper and the mechanics of printing presses, a Web designer will need a deep understanding of the inner workings of Web technologies.

The Web is a medium of constraint—designers new to the Web are shocked at the limitations they face in order to practice their craft. However, the technology is changing, and thus the approach to how we put Web interfaces together is changing. This chapter will delve into the biggest issue facing designers today—the shift from "pixel-based" design to "rule-based" design. No longer can designers simply pass off a Photoshop sketch to production assistants and ask them to make the page. Now, designers have to exploit the very nature of the Web—that there is no such thing as a controlled user environment—and make their designs react accordingly. Designers are creating rules for their pages, building in constraints and behaviors, so that their creations mold to the environment in which they're displayed. This relates directly to the discussion in the first chapter: Without a fundamental understanding of how presentational aspects of a solid Web product interact with the behavioral, there is no hope for success.

I have had the good fortune to work with some incredible designers throughout the past few years. I've been consistently awed by how good designers can create normalcy out of chaos; how they can clearly communicate ideas through the organizing and manipulating of words and pictures. I've also been amazed at how often those outside the discipline of design assume that what designers do is decoration—likely because so much bad design simply *is* decoration. Good design isn't. Good design is problem solving.

It is easy to say that the Web has been revolutionary—that the Web has changed everything, that we're living in a new networked world with a new networked economy; that traditional thinking is bad, and that just because something is different it is good. That, I'm afraid, isn't true. Rather, the Web is a lens that magnifies and modifies everything we see. Shopping is different when viewed through this lens. But it is still shopping. E-mail has fundamentally changed how we communicate with one another and how businesses get their work done. But it is still communication and business.

The same goes for design. Viewed through the lens of the Web, the nature of design is very different, and in this chapter we'll talk about how. But it is still design. We have hundreds of years of tradition to fall back on when uncovering the foundations of communication through a visual medium. We don't need to reinvent the basic relationships between ideas and layout, between communication and visual representation. These rules developed over countless years, and continue to evolve. We need to understand them. It is one of the crucial steps to becoming a good designer.

Yet, just because a designer may be proficient at creating magazine spreads doesn't mean that designer can draw blueprints for a skyscraper. A friend of mine designs cars for Chrysler. He can tell me more detail about the human factors of dashboard instrumentation than I thought possible. Does that make him a good Web designer as well? Probably not. If he chose to change his career path, he may have an advantage—automobile design is a pure blend of form and function married with inherent appreciation for current style and marketing. Those skills would apply well to what we do on the Web. But that would only be a head start, not the unquestioned assumption that he would succeed at creating interfaces for the Web product.

The same theory applies to print designers. Recently, a colleague posted to a design mailing list expressing frustration with a designer with whom he was working. This designer had a strong print background, and was skilled in visual communication and graphic art. Yet she refused to "limit" herself with an understanding of HTML. Her reasoning was interesting: She felt that by tying her hands with the technology of the Web, she would be unable to create innovative designs. She felt that knowing the medium would limit her creativity.

I call this approach to Web design "Burying Your Head in the Sand." When I first started working at *Wired* magazine, I remember having a long talk with the creative directors about their process. They were doing amazing things with print design back then—eight-color printing, metallic and florescent inks. You know how they were able to get such amazing results? A deep knowledge of the technology behind print design. They could go on and on talking about dot gain with ink X on paper stock Y and how this would work in natural light but not through the monitors we had available at the time. They could relate the results of countless tests they'd run on the press that printed the magazine. I couldn't imagine them saying, "Oh, I don't need to know anything about printing. That will just limit my creativity."

Can we imagine the same thinking on the Web? It's a complicated and tenuous balance. On one hand, one of the reasons many early Web sites were successful can be traced to a rebellion of sorts. HTML was exceedingly limited, especially when compared to the rich graphic tools available to designers accustomed to print work. As a result, early Web designers pushed back hard on the basic limitations of the Web. While some bemoaned the "decoration" of a "rich hypertext system," others demanded a Web that would accommodate art *and* science. The results were often stunning examples of visual design created as pure hacks to the original intentions of HTML and the Web.

But like I said, it's more complicated than that. It would be easy to continue to bury our heads in the sand and ignore the limitations of even today's Web. But effective Web designers will also have a deep knowledge of the technology behind the products they are creating. They will understand the fundamental possibilities and limitations of the Web. In the first chapter, we looked at the interaction between presentation, structure, and behavior in Web products and Web teams. I suggested that the best designers were the ones that mastered their particular discipline, but were also multidisciplinary enough to comprehend what each corner of the triangle was capable of.

It's time to turn our attention to behavior—the dynamic nature of the Web and how it works.

Rule-Based Design

You cannot tell how your Web site will look on other people's screens.

There. I said it. And it's true. No matter how much control you are used to when designing for other media, you're going to have to give up some of it if you want to be successful on the Web. Compare that to designing for print. Designers of traditional printed material have complete control over virtually every aspect of their output. They can choose inks, paper stock, printing method, image resolution, color values, type treatments, and alignment down to a hundredth of a point.

Web sites, on the other hand, have variables where print has absolutes. When Web designers finish a page, the representation of that design on their screen is only one possible variation of millions that are possible. The difference, of course, is in the distribution. Print designers create a physical object—a book or magazine or catalog—and send that object to their audience. They know exactly what is going out.

Conversely, Web designers send the source code—they send the words and pictures and scripts and structure. Their audiences then use a computer with a browser to assemble the end product and display it. Nothing physical ships from producer to consumer. Hence the variables. When the Web page is reassembled on the user's end of the wire, all manner of change can happen. The user will have a different size monitor with different resolution, color representation, and gamma settings. The user may or may not have the same fonts installed. There may even be a different browser or operating system waiting for the page, introducing a thousand other variables.

Steve Champeon's "A Jaundiced Eye" in Netscape Navigator 6.0 rendering correctly with support for CSS.

To illustrate this discrepancy, let's take a look at the visual appearance of a Web site in a series of browsers—we'll leave out the different devices for now. Steve Champeon's "A Jaundiced Eye" at `http://a.jaundicedeye.com/` is a good example, since Champeon designed the interface to degrade across different versions of different browsers. Below, the page is shown in a browser with some of the most advanced support for things like the Cascading Stylesheet standard: the beta version of Netscape Navigator 6.0.

Look at the subtle details in this version of the design. The dashed borders around the individual items, and the spacing between the paragraphs. Now look at the design in a different browser: Microsoft's Internet Explorer 5.0.

Notice the differences? Internet Explorer doesn't support all of CSS, so effects like the dashed border don't show up in this interface. It's still workable—

The same Web site in a slightly less standards-compliant browser, Internet Explorer 5.0.

in fact, it's probably safe to suggest that most users wouldn't notice the difference at all. But it's not what Champeon had specified in his code. The browser did a good job at trying to get close to the intended rendering, but since it couldn't, the design now looks different for different visitors to this Web site. Let's see the page in an even less sophisticated browser: Netscape Navigator 4.08.

The page with even fewer supported features as shown in Navigator 4.08.

Here the page really starts to look different. Navigator 4.08 just barely attempts to support Cascading Stylesheets, and implements much of it incorrectly. The result is a page that misses out on many of the design elements Champeon intended. The borders are gone now, and many of the items are misaligned. Compare this to the first screenshot of the page, and think back to our print design analogy. If a designer had intended for the first, but seen the second coming off the press, would that be acceptable? I'd guess probably not. But is this lack of consistency appropriate on the Web? Only if you are anticipating the results.

Finally, let's look at the page in a text-only browser, in this case Lynx on a machine running the Linux operating system. The page looks nothing like it did in the graphical browsers, but to Champeon's credit, it is still quite usable. The content can be read, and something of the overall structure is noticeable. The more vain Web designers among us may shudder to think of their pages being displayed so coarsely, but this may very well be the only way some users can get to the content. At least they can see *something*.

The page as rendered in the text-only browser, Lynx.

This all boils down to one simple axiom: You must design for variables.

Postmodern thinker Derrida suggested that there were no absolutes—that all truths were based on interpretation and therefore all perception was relative. Derrida would have loved the Web. Your fonts won't work. Your colors will look different. Your scripts may break. Your design may not even show up. Nothing you see on your screen is absolute. How do we cope with this postmodern nightmare?

Embrace the technology, don't fight it.

The Black Magic of Web Typography

Even the simplest <FONT> tag reveals this maxim. The tag allows for rudimentary control over the typography of a document, allowing control over what typeface is selected, at what size it should be rendered, and in what color the type should appear. Simple enough—especially considering HTML's bizarre limitation of only seven type sizes. Yet even this deceptively simple addition to our Web design toolkit gets us into trouble.

You probably already know that selecting what typeface should be used to display some text is accomplished by the following:

```
<FONT FACE="typeface">
```

But what you enter for "typeface" depends on what your users have installed on their systems. In other words, something as fundamental to design as selecting a typeface is *completely variable* and dependent on an external. Stated yet again: You have no control.

So, for the following to work on your Web page:

```
<FONT FACE="Verdana">
```

means that your users will need to have the typeface Verdana installed on their systems. And what if they don't? Then your page will be rendered in the default typeface for the user's browser, usually some variant of Times Roman. But if they do, then all is fine. How can you know for sure that your pages are appearing the way you intended? The answer again: You can't be sure.

The developers who came up with the <FONT> tag saw this basic limitation and offered a bit of relief. They allowed for a series of font families to be specified, and they programmed the browsers to use the first one the user's system had available. So instead of pinning all your hopes on your users having Verdana installed, you can provide a sort of safety net with this code:

```
<FONT FACE="Verdana, Arial, Helvetica, sans-serif">
```

Now, when a user views your page, they will see the text inside this tag as Verdana if it's installed. If not, the browser will look for Arial. Still not there? On to Helvetica. And if none of these faces are present on the user's computer system, then the browser will find any san-serif typeface and simply use that. The browser continues from the most specific to the most general, progressively searching for a typeface—any typeface—that will come close to what you actually intended.

HTML is filled with little fallbacks like this. It's all part of a basic philosophy of degrading gracefully across all platforms and browsers. We'll talk more about this in Chapter Five, "Browsers."

I bring this up now for an entirely different reason. This bit of haggling we're forced to do with typography is a great example of the control we give up as Web designers. And it points to the first major lesson when dealing with the behavior of Web pages: The shift from pixel-based design to rule-based design.

Getting Liquid

You can see designers struggling with the lack of control every where you look online. How many times have you come to a Web site only to be confronted with a screen of instructions. "This Web site is best viewed with Browser X version N on a 800 by 600 or higher resolution screen set to thousands of colors."

This "Best Viewed with" mentality is thankfully becoming a thing of the past, albeit slowly. Most commercial Web sites have finally realized that the best way to serve their audience is to get out of the way and let them accomplish what they came to do. Still, there is a vestige of designers who continue to demand that *users* conform to *their* whims. This is a holdover from the old method of design, which I talked about earlier—the notion of designing physical objects that get distributed to users. They are, in essence, attempting to package a pixel-perfect picture of their Web site and ship it off to their audience—again, a control issue.

The "Best Viewed with" design approach leads to other hacks as well. These sites are filled with text set in graphic files—another attempt to exert control over typography. And while the control may appear to work in the short term, the result is a Web site that cannot be searched, indexed, translated, or otherwise manipulated. It's a losing battle.

As we saw in the <FONT> example above, we can start to abandon the absolutes of traditional design and move towards a more *rule-based* approach. Rather than spending countless hours sweating over individual pixels, we should turn our attention to how page elements behave. Designers who embrace the technology of the Web are creating interfaces that respond to the environment in which they are displayed. These rules take the form of visual suggestions rather than maxims. "This headline should be set in Verdana if it is available, but can scale through these other choices if that face is not available. In fact, use a sans-serif face if nothing else is installed on my users' machines."

Page layout is another good example of absolutes versus variables. I'm often asked what size screen we design for. "All of them," I say with only a hint of self-righteousness. It's true, though. Just as with the variability of typography, the resolution of my users' screens can be frustratingly unpredictable. Even if I could anticipate every monitor size in existence, how do I deal with the infinite possibilities for sizing their actual browser window?

How I cope with this dilemma is telling. I could demand users yank their window out to the size I require for my layout, or I could build layouts that respond to any size. One way to accomplish this is by simply using relative values when defining my layout, creating "liquid pages." Let me explain.

Web pages are often designed using HTML tables for layout. While this may not have been the intent of the architects of the language, there are certain advantages to using tables to position elements on the page. Tables follow a set of heuristics for how they take up screen real estate when displaying your page. The individual cells of a table will expand to accommodate their contents. By doing so, the effect is one of dependencies—each cell is constrained by both its contents, and also by the contents of the adjoining cells in the same row and column. Add to this the ability for cells to span multiple rows or columns, and you get a sophisticated method of developing page layouts. Especially when you consider this key fact: Cells can take a percentage value for their width.

How does this relate to rule-based design? Easy. I've already talked about how we're going to let the user's environment determine the layout of a page. So by creating a table that contains percentage values, you are essentially letting the user set the layout of the page to be whatever fits the browser window the most efficiently. Look at this example:

```
<TABLE>
  <TR>
    <TD WIDTH="20%">Page Navigation</TD>
    <TD WIDTH="80%">Page Contents</TD>
  </TR>
</TABLE>
```

Type that into an HTML page and view it in a browser, and you'll see a two-column, page layout that expands and contracts as you resize the window—a liquid page. Imagine a column of navigational links taking up 20 percent of the left side of the page, and paragraphs of content filling up the other 80 percent on the right.

It's a simple example, but one that gives us a glimpse of a whole system of rules that could be put in place for a particular page layout. The navigation, for example, could be locked to a specific width, while the content area could be flexible. If this were being developed for a commercial site, ad units could float to the right moving with the edge of the browser. Margins could be created around a document and dynamically scaled with the size of the window, and on and on.

On Stating the Obvious (`stating.theobvious.com`), Michael Sippey uses a similar technique to create a liquid layout. His interface is one of minimalist elegance. An unobtrusive brand logo coupled with a careful eye for type leads to an inviting and intelligent page layout. This layout is also a great example of the ease at which pages can become liquid with a few simple tweaks to the underlying code.

Michael Sippey's "Stating the Obvious" uses a very simple table structure to accomplish a liquid design.

By looking at the source, we can see the overall structure of the page is made up of two simple tables, one with the logo and navigation, another with the contents of the page. Both tables are set to a relative value, in this case they both ask for 100 percent of the width of the page. The top table uses this code to accomplish its goal:

```
<table width="100%" border=0 cellpadding=0 cellspacing=0>
  <tr>
    <td valign=top align=left width="1%">
      <!-- logo image -->
    </td>
    <td valign=bottom align=right>
      <!-- Navigation links -->
      <hr color="#C0C0C0" size=1 noshade>
    </td>
  </tr>
</table>
```

While far from complicated, the code does include a couple of interesting tricks. The table cells (defined with the `<td>` tags) have no absolute size set for them. However, the left cell is essentially fixed to the width of the graphic it contains. By giving that cell a width of one percent, the cell will try to be as small as it can possibly get. Yet, the browser can't make the cell any smaller than the image file within, so that part of the table gets what is essentially a fixed width. The other cell has no width at all, and therefore takes the rest of the available page. Under the navigation links, Sippey has added a Horizontal Rule (`<hr>`), which is set to render in a specific gray that matches the logo (`"#C0C0C0"`), and without any shadow effects (`noshade`). Again, no width is specified for this element, with the result being a visual element that figures its width on its own.

Under the navigation, the page's content fits into a similar table structure, but this time reversed. Sippey accomplishes a liquid layout again using this code:

```
<table width="100%" border=0 cellpadding=0 cellspacing=0>
  <tr>
    <td width=75 valign=top align=right></td>
    <td valign=top align=left>
      <!-- page content -->
    </td>
    <td width=30 valign=top align=right></td>
    <td width=170 valign=top align=right>
      <!-- commerce links -->
    </td>
  </tr>
</table>
```

The page is made up of two content cells: one containing the page's content, the other with a few links to recommended media items. Yet, the actual table structure has two additional cells, one with a width of 75, the other with a width of 130. These two cells, while devoid of any actual content, are essentially acting as margins for the content. They are a fixed width, as is the commerce cell, giving a fairly rigid construction to the page. The center cell—the one with the actual content in it—has no width set. Rather, like the navigation in the table above, this cell is left to take the rest of the browser window's available real estate.

The effect is nice. The page feels sized correctly no matter how big or small your browser window is… to a point. Scaling down the window too far creates an incredibly narrow column for the text of the page. One way to deal with this is to add a physical constraint to the relatively sized column. Much like the logo graphic in the top table of this page, we could insert an image into the content column of the lower table and give it a width that would define how small we would allow the column to get. Since this page is working just fine without the addition of another visual element, we could just use a transparent GIF image no bigger than a single pixel, and stretch it using height and width tags to the desired size. The code we used before would now look like this:

```
<table width="100%" border=0 cellpadding=0 cellspacing=0>
  <tr>
    <td width=75 valign=top align=right></td>
    <td valign=top align=left>
      <img src="spacer.gif" height=1 width=250
alt="spacer">
      <br>
      <!-- page content -->
      etc.
```

Now, when the browser is resized to the point where the center column would be smaller than 250 pixels, the cell bumps against the invisible spacer image, and is constrained to that size. There are drawbacks to this strategy, though. The image may be negligibly small, but it requires a request to the server, which can slow things down a bit. It may also be considered bad form to constrain *any* part of the user experience, especially with a hack like a single-pixel image. I find it a fair compromise. Users get a flexible representation of the interface, while designers can maintain a certain level of visual control over how their pages are rendered.

Without any sort of constraint, a liquid interface can get too wide or narrow.

A Liquid Application

This functionality need not be limited to tables, either. Page layouts using frames can also take relative values for the height or width of certain regions. Frames can be sized either with percentage values like tables, or with the use of an asterisk. This syntax tells the browser to simply use whatever real estate is left over. So...

```
<FRAMESET cols="100,*,100" >
<FRAME src="myNavigation.html">
  <FRAME src="myDocument.html">
  <FRAME src="thirdColumn.html">
</FRAMESET>
```

simply means that the browser should draw three frames:
two 100 pixel columns fixed at the edges of the page, and
one that takes up however many pixels are left in the center
of the browser window—again, a liquid design.

The examples above, however, are only glimpses into
what is possible within the context of liquid design. Let's
look at a real-world example.

Kvetch.com is fun. It also, from time to time, can be a
little troubling.

The site was designed as a virtual outlet for folks to let
off a little steam. Anonymous users can post just about anything they're angry about to the site. Interested voyeurs can
peek into any of a half dozen subject areas to see the outra-
geous postings. It's interesting, in a twisted sort of way.

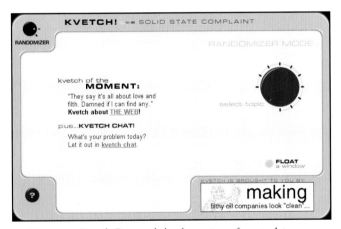

Designer Derek Powazek built an interface to his
kvetch.com project that would approximate a sort of "com-
plaint application." The site looks as if it is a control panel
that would exist in the real world—the edges of the interface are curved and lit by a distinctive light source.

Controls for the site are rendered as buttons that are turned by clicking, with an indicator that rotates as a selection is made.

Where the interface departs from real world physics is its ability to resize itself to the current browser window.

Kvetch.com uses a fairly complicated set of nested frames to allow liquidity both horizontally and vertically. By setting some frames with absolute values and others with percentages, Powazek can determine just what should expand and collapse, while controlling the overall effect in place.

Little images placed in key locations give the Kvetch.com interface the illusion of reality. Rendered with a consistent light source, the edges of the screen give off a gleaming appearance, while spinning indicator knobs show off the site's functionality.

Naturally, to achieve this effect, the borders of the frames have been set to "0." However, let's turn them on for a second to see just how the interface is being composed. We should be able to get a glimpse of how a liquid page actually comes together.

Kvetch is made up of a frameset containing three rows. Each row is then cut into individual frames. This creates a

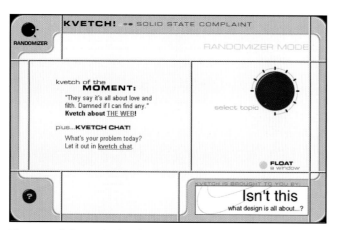

grid of interface regions that can be manipulated with precision to create a design that scales appropriately. Here, you can see how the rows are divided to make up the overall page.

Then, within the top and bottom row, the corner pieces are

The overall frameset for the Kvetch.com interface is made up of three rows. Each row has unique characteristics that in sum make up a liquid page.

given absolute dimensions. They stay locked down, grounding the interface to the corners of the browser windows.

Then, each row in the interface includes relatively sized pieces to allow the design to scale in the correct direction. The top and bottom rows include horizontally scaling frames, while the middle row contains vertically scaling pieces. The overall effect is a sort of dynamic picture frame that surrounds the page's content no matter what size the browser.

The corners of the interface stay rigidly sized.

Finally, the center of the page contains a frame that scales in both directions, with a relatively sized table inside that expands and contracts to fit the space left by the surrounding frame. The result is a perfectly scaled interface no matter what size the browser window.

These rules, as interesting as they may be to play with, are still very simple. All we're doing is addressing certain areas of a page layout, but nothing more complex.

But, we also haven't added the elegance of Cascading Stylesheets to this discussion.

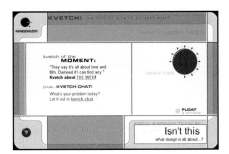

Building the scalable picture frame with relatively sized edge pieces.

Getting Relative with CSS

Thinking back to Chapter One, you'll recall our conversation about the structure, presentation, and behavior of Web pages. I bring up the triangle metaphor again because we're going to see just how flexible it is.

Remember how I explained the multidisciplinary nature of our model? Designers, for example, need to be experts in the design corner of

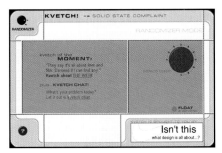

Filling the rest of the screen with the center frame and a relatively sized table.

the triangle. But they also need to branch out and explore the possibilities of other disciplines. Our conversation so far about behavior has been almost entirely about style. And that's fine. The relationship between how something looks and how something works can and should be blurred. It only makes sense that the functional and aesthetic qualities of anything—but especially Web designs—be intimately bound.

Let's look at an example of this relationship through developing the behavior of a liquid page by manipulating its style. We'll start with an old typographic axiom: The most readable line lengths for a paragraph are "an alphabet and a half." This means that for maximum legibility in a chunk of content, each line in a paragraph should be roughly 40 characters wide.

How does this interact with our goal of a liquid page? After all, if we set up a page that behaves by filling the screen, we'll loose control of our line lengths, thereby letting go of legibility. Can we have both? Possibly.

First, we'll start by abandoning the notion of a fixed font size. CSS gives us lots of typographic control, as we saw in Chapter Two. But it also gives us some new units of measurement, most notably the *em unit.*

Unlike points or pixels, which represent an absolute size for elements defined by them, the em is based on the font—technically, 1em is meant to represent the width of the lowercase "m" character in whatever font you're using. Most browsers aren't this sophisticated, though, and actually just define 1em as the "default" size. Thus, in Internet Explorer version 4 and higher, the typeface Verdana set to 1em would render as 12pt. However, this isn't a rigid 12pt, but rather the base of whatever the user has set as the default. So if I increase my font size in the browser (using the preferences) to 16pt as the default, then 1em becomes 16pt and everything will scale accordingly.

Now, you may argue that the majority of users never change their preferences. And you'd be right. Netscape made more money selling advertising on its home page (which came up by default in users' browsers) than from anything else. However, we're attempting to build pages that serve all of our users, no matter how they view our pages. I can't tell you how many times I've tried to read documentation at 3AM after a marathon day of developing, and cursed the designer who fixed the point size to an absolute value. So much for my tired eyes.

Anyway, we're going to start with some text set to 10pt for our page copy. To approximate this, I do the math: if 1em = 12pt, then .8em = 9.6pt, which the browser will round up for us, keeping our code simpler. I'll use this as the basis for the entire document by putting this in my stylesheet:

```
body {font-size: .8em; font-family: "Times New Roman",
Times, serif; }
```

Now, every element on the page I'm creating will inherit the font size and font family information that I've set up for the <BODY>. By setting up my style this way, I can simply change the individual characteristics for each element as they relate to the overall document. Every part of the page can and should be related to one base unit—a base unit that is set based on my users' preferences.

Let's move on. To incorporate our design axiom of an alphabet and a half, we'll set up our content. Since 1em is essentially one character, setting the width of my paragraphs to 40em will give me the ideal line length.

```
P {width: 40em; }
```

I'd like to lighten up the visual weight of each paragraph as well, so I'll increase the leading by setting the line-length property to a comfortable value. And, I'd like to start with about a one inch left margin, so with 1em as 12 points, and knowing that there are roughly 72 points in an inch, I can set the margins to 72 divided by 12, or 6em.

```
P {width: 40 em; line-length: 1.4em; margin-left: 6em }
```

Inheritance is working for us now. The paragraph is contained within the body, and therefore inherits all the typographic settings. So our paragraphs will be set in Verdana (or whatever else is available) and will be rendered at 10pt.

No need to stop with text. I can set the height and width of images to similar values. I'd like a 3-inch by 1-inch logo at the top of the page, so I'll define it through a class in my stylesheet.

```
IMG.logo {height: 6em; width: 18em; }
```

You can probably guess by now what the effect will be on my page. In a browser with default preferences, my logo will be 3-inch by 1-inch in the corner of the page. It will look balanced against the surrounding type and white space that I've carefully designed. However, if a user decides to bump up the font size, my entire page will react to that setting now. Paragraphs will not only have bigger text, but get wider as well. The margins and leading will readjust to an appropriately scaled size to match the new font size. And my images will stay in the proper proportion, since they've been set to relative values as well. The entire page is responding to both my desires as the designer, but also to the unique and individual preferences of my myriad users.

Contrast this to the "best viewed with" method of design we talked about earlier. Rather than demand that everyone who views my page conform to my screen resolution or browser width or type standards, I'm creating pages that meet my users half way. It's compromise without adversely effecting the visual communication inherent in the design process. My pages have been imbued with behavior—they can almost act autonomously, while still under my control.

It's Web design the way it was intended to be.

From Scripts to Screenplays

In what now seems like a past life, I used to be the managing editor of a series of small community newspapers. We did stories on car crashes and Little League scores and weddings and city council meetings—with a staff of five. So, besides being managing editor, I also reported and wrote stories, took the occasional photograph and laid out all the pages of the paper. Laying out newspapers can be fun, until you get to the headlines. Writing and sizing headlines can be as invigorating as writing haiku all day long—interesting for a while, but eventually degrading into tedium. The words of the headlines, you see, had to match the width of the columns in the stories. With fairly narrow columns and typically constrained headlines, the job became one of constant word play. Wouldn't it be wonderful, I would dream, if I could have a machine that did this for me?

In the CSS example above, I've developed a series of dependencies on the typographic characteristics of the <BODY> tag—essentially a series of absolute rules that can be modified through preferences by my users. But what if the values set on the <BODY> tag were *truly* relative. What if I didn't even know what they were? Could I create a script that effectively encapsulated the dreary work I used to do at the newspaper?

We're about to modify the example above to create a design that should feel right no matter what environmental variables are at play. So far, we've accounted for the width of the browser window when scaling table cells, and the user preferences for setting font size. Now I'll put them together and add scripting to dynamically size page elements based on a slew of variable factors.

The more you explore the behavior of Web pages, the more you'll have to occasionally dip into scripting to achieve the effects you're after. As I've said, the interdisciplinary nature of the Web requires us to branch out as far as we can towards the other domains. We're going to be using JavaScript to manipulate the visual appearance of our pages.

One of the wonderful features of Web scripting languages like JavaScript is the ability to peer into our users' worlds. Thus, I can gain access to things like the default values of many things: What browser they are using, what plugins are installed, and even useful data like the screen resolution and browser window width. The latter are particularly interesting. If I can tell what size the screen is and how wide the browser is on that screen, I should be able to lay out pages based on that knowledge.

To get the window width to lay out our page, we're going to have to ask using the native language of the browser. This language—the vocabulary used to address each and every aspect and element of a particular page—is called the Document Object Model, or DOM. The DOM is really just a shorthand notation for asking the browser questions like, "Hey, what color is the fourth paragraph on this page?" Or, in my example, "I need to know the current width of the browser window in pixels." Here's how I ask that question using JavaScript:

```
var mySize = document.body.offsetWidth;
```

This little bit of code sets up a variable for us named "mySize," into which we dump the width of the current browser window. More specifically, we'll get the width of the *canvas*, or the number of visible horizontal pixels displayed in the user's current window.

Now, we can do some simple calculations to derive a font size. In the example below, a typical news story from the Wired News Web site, I've used this algorithm to set the size of the headline:

```
<script>
  var mySize = document.body.offsetWidth/29;
  headline.style.fontSize = mySize;
</script>
```

Let's look at what's going on here. First, we're dealing with a page that's been set up with a liquid structure. The logo and header are locked to the top of the screen, and sized at 100%, to fill up the entire window. Then, the story sits in a table cell between two columns—an empty margin

and a collection of narrow advertising units. The two outer columns are locked to an absolute width, while the story fills the remaining space. Thus, the layout is responding to the variable width of the user's browser.

The headline, however, is what we're going to change. The text itself is rendered with this structural code:

```
<H1 id="headline">Riffage Buys SF Concert Hall</H1>
```

and this style code:

```
<style>
  body {font-size: .8em; font-family: Verdana, Arial,
    Geneva, sans-serif}
  H1 {font-family: Verdana, Arial, Helvetica, san-serif;
    font-weight: bold;}
</style>
```

Combining the structure, style, and behavior, we get a dynamically sized headline. The JavaScript code takes the width of the canvas by asking the browser for it by way of

the document.body.offsetWidth node in the DOM. But
before I assign it to a variable, I need to massage it a bit. If
we simply set the size of the headline to the width of the
browser window, it would be enormous. So to scale it down
a bit, I'm dividing this particular headline, "Riffage Buys SF
Concert Hall," by 29 to get it roughly the right size to fit
the width of the column of text. So when the browser is set
to, say, 750 pixels wide, that number gets divided by 29 and
I'm left with 26 pixels after rounding. In the last line of the
script, I simply tell the browser to look for an element with
the ID of "headline" (which I had already applied to my
`<H1>`), and set its font-size attribute to whatever is in the
`mySize` variable. In one fell swoop, I've grabbed the window
width, scaled it down, and applied it to my headline. At
that size, the headline fits atop the story just fine. All we
need to do is find an event to trigger the script.

Since I want this resizing event to happen instantly
when the page loads, I'll create a function, and call that
function with an `onLoad` event on the body tag. Since I also
want the script to resize my headline as the browser resizes,
I'll fire the function from that event, as well:

```
<script>
  function change_size() {
    var mySize = document.body.offsetWidth/29;
    headline.style.fontSize = mySize;
  }
</script>
...
<body onLoad="change_size()" onResize="change_size()">
```

Here's where it starts to get really interesting. If I were to
resize the browser window, not only would the column of
text get narrower, but the headline would resize itself pro-
portionately to fit. Likewise, as the browser gets larger, the
column widens, and the headline grows bigger and bigger.

Constraining Myself

Of course, we still want to exert some amount of design control over our presentation. Once you start playing around with dynamically sized elements like our headline example above, you quickly realize how ridiculous the extremes are. For example, if you scale the window down to a very small size, suddenly the headline is completely illegible. And you can see why: If the window gets below, say, 100 pixels, our math begins to fall apart. 100 divided by 29 is just over 3. Three-pixel type is, to say the least, not the easiest to read on the screen. We need some constraints.

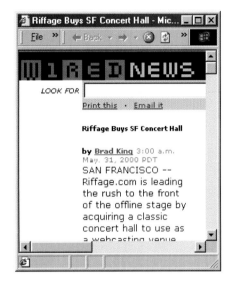

To set limits on the scaling of type, I'm going to add a bit of a reality check to the script that sizes the headline. Before actually applying my derived value to the font-size of the headline, I'm going to see if it is either too small or too big. I'll do this with a couple of if...else statements—a common programming technique for adding logic to code.

```
<script>
  function change_size() {
    var mySize = document.body.offsetWidth/29;
    if (mySize < 14) {
      mySize = 14;
    } else (mySize > 50) {
      mysize = 50;
    }
    headline.style.fontSize = mySize;
  }
</script>
```

While this may seem to be getting complicated, it really isn't. The new lines above simply tell the browser, "If the value you're about to use to set the headline's font size is less than 14 pixels, then set the value to 14. If it's bigger than 50 pixels, then just use 50." Now I can rest assured that my headline will never get too small to read or ridiculously big. I've set up a dynamic—yet constrained—system for displaying a nicely fitting headline on my story.

Knowing Even Less

I'm getting close to my goal now—a machine that will format my headlines for me. There is still one variable left to deal with, and it's a big one. While the script we've been developing so far has accounted for screen-width column size, as well as set up constraints for big and small extremes, we still need to tackle one fundamental unknown: the headline itself.

Wired News, like most other content-heavy Web sites, doesn't actually server HTML files when you visit its pages. Rather, all the content for all the stories is stored in a large and fairly complicated database. These stories are pulled out of this database, and then pushed through a publishing system that almost magically creates the pages you see in your browser. We'll get into the nuts and bolts of this process in Chapter Eight, "Object-Oriented Publishing" because now I'm still focused on formatting that headline.

You see, all of the powerful behind-the-scenes technology puts designers in a unique predicament. I've been talking about how everything we've dealt with thus far has been relative. Just how little we know about the environment to which we send our designs is turning out to be a sort of postmodern nightmare free of any absolute truths whatsoever. And now for the ultimate—after accounting for the wide variety of user systems and complex preferences, the sad truth: *I don't even know what my headline will be*.

That's right. I have no idea how many words or characters will be in that string of text. Sure, we can put constraints on our editors and ensure they write headlines with some manner of consistency. But ultimately, the hundreds of stories that flow through the newsroom and onto the site are going to do so automatically. They are going to come barreling out of a database and into a template, but it will happen at the speed of light and without so much as a quick glance from a designer. I therefore need to set up a system that will deal not only with the constraints my users will place on the design, but also with content I've never seen. How do I account for this?

Time to add a couple more lines of code to my script. I've already set the size dynamically, and added my constraints. Now, I'll do what I used to do at the newspaper: I'll tweak the size based on the available headline.

Once the text comes out of the database and is married to the template, my script will be able to ask the computer for one final and crucial piece of information: Just how long is that headline? I'll ask this question with these two simple lines of code:

```
var myHead = headline.innerHTML;
var targetSize = myHead.length;
```

I'm adding a couple of new variables to the script here. The first, myHead, uses a bit of the Document Object Model to look for that element with the ID of headline, and grab its contents. So, in our example from earlier, the value for myHead would be set to "Riffage to Buy SF Music Venue." So now, even though I don't know what the headline will be, when the page is finally rendered at least my script will. The next line sets a variable named targetSize to the length of the string; or, in English, the total number of letters and spaces in the headline. With this information, we can modify the algorithm that sets the font-size property of the headline to look like this:

```
mySize = (document.body.offsetWidth/targetSize) * 1.35;
```

Now the final size of the headline will be calculated by taking the number of pixels in the current browser window, and dividing by the number of characters in my headline. You'll remember that earlier I was simply dividing by 27. Again, we're replacing an absolute value with a relative one. So with a browser window at, say, 750 pixels and the headline from our earlier example coming in at 29 character, we're left with a font size of 25.8 pixels. To get the font size to match the specific column in this layout, I need it to be about 135 percent of what this math gives me, so I've added the multiplication at the end. I take my 25.8pixel value and run it up to 34.9pixels and now, as if by magic, my headline fits atop the column of text as if I'd designed it from scratch to look just right. If our headline happened to be 23 characters and the window was scaled out to 825 pixels wide, we'd end up with 825 divided by 23, then multiplied by 1.35 to give me a size of 48.2 pixels, which also fits just fine. And all the while, if my users scale their browsers too big or too small, I can keep that headline between 16 and 50 pixels using the if... then constraints I added earlier.

Here now is the completed script:

```
<script>
  function change_size() {
    var myHead = headline.innerHTML;
    var targetSize = myHead.length;
    var mySize = (document.body.offsetWidth/targetSize)*1.35;
    if (mySize < 14) {
      mySize = 14;
    } else if (mySize > 50) {
      mySize = 50;
    }
    headline.style.fontSize = mySize;
  }
</script>
```

And you can see how it works in these screenshots of our story with a variety of headlines:

The script is resizing each headline based not only on the available space, but according to how many characters is in each one. Now, any headline will fit with any column width—a truly liquid page.

Building the Virtual Designer

I didn't include this script in this chapter to give you a working example of how to create scalable headlines. In fact, this script uses some proprietary additions to the DOM included by Microsoft in their Internet Explorer browser. Using it in other browsers like Netscape Navigator will cause an obtuse error message to appear. I included it here—and spent the time deconstructing every last detail— to show you how designers are going to have to evolve to embrace the behavior of Web pages as well as the technology behind those behaviors. A good eye will remain mandatory in the discipline. A designer's deep understanding of the fundamentals of visual communication will never go away. But much like a magazine designer's knowledge of inks on paper and the mechanics of printing presses, a Web designer will need a deep understanding of the inner workings of Web technologies.

This script, then, is an example of a much bigger idea. Throughout this chapter, we've been looking at examples of rule-based design, and how the traditional notion of pixel-based design is rapidly being left behind. But here's the big picture: Good designers are harnessing the technology available to them and using it to encode the process they use to do good design. A pixel-based designer spends time sizing a headline perfectly to an absolute column and page width. A rule-based designer spends time converting that task to a browser-based script.

In our example, I converted one design process for sizing headlines into one script that does it for me. Now imagine the myriad other design decisions that a news story page may need. I've only scratched the surface of page layout, branding, advertising, internal and external navigation, and everything else that falls into that particular page. Extrapolate even further to different pages on the site, and then to the many different types of sites—what rules would need to be encoded for a search engine, or an e-commerce shopping cart, or a stock portfolio tracking application, or an artist's portfolio, or anything else?

Go Build It

I just walked you through a very detailed description of a fairly simple bit of JavaScript. It's important to remember that what the script was doing is much more interesting that how it accomplished the task. And that's what I want you to focus on. Can you communicate the functionality of a particular design goal with the developers on your team? Or will you dig into the syntax and fundamentals of the various Web technologies and produce the behavior of Web pages yourself? The answer will be different for every design and every designer, but each will be somewhere on that technical continuum.

Regardless, at least we'll all know how to get our hands dirty and our heads out of the sand.

Chapter Five

Browsers

Just as your watch keeps time, your telephone calls other phones, and your stereo accepts all compact discs, so too should all browsers show all Web pages.

[5]

The infamous browser wars have taken their toll. Not only is the installed base of

clients completely fractured between old versions and competing vendors, but

each browser has its own bugs and peculiarities. For the hapless Web designer,

the outlook is bleak. Do I have to make multiple versions of my site? How can I

afford to do that? Am I resigned to a lowest-common-denominator version of my

brilliant design ideas? This chapter digs into the reasons why the browsers are so

different, how Web developers can form a strategy for dealing with this mess, and

what basic techniques they can use to develop around the lack of support for

basic standards. Finally, we'll look at what we can do to help fix this, and how

the browser makers are responding.

Isn't it amazing that the Internet works? It's easy to forget that sometimes. We sit at our computers using our browsers with e-mail applications in the background, communicating effortlessly with computers around the world. We take for granted that we can fire off a message to virtually anyone and they will be able to read it. Yet, that works only because of the protocols beneath the surface, all glued together in a fantastic network of connectivity.

Thankfully, most of us don't have to muck around with the underlying code that makes the Internet function; we can keep all that complexity abstract by using our windows and wizards. In fact, we're so far removed from the underlying protocols that we can completely forget that the Internet isn't really a physical thing, but simply a collection of standards to which everyone has agreed. Without standards, though, there would be no Internet. The Internet *is* standards.

Why, then, are we having such a difficult time with the Web? The arguments and politics of Web standards have raged behind the scenes almost since the birth of the first browsers.

Recently, there has been an increased focus on the standards—or, rather, the lack of *compliance* with standards—that have helped popularize the Web and make it a commodity of daily life. From a grassroots level, developers have begun to air their frustrations with the lack of basic interoperability between browsers—or even versions of the same browser. "Why is this so hard?" they ask. "Why do I have to spend so much time getting my pages to work on every browser?"

The timing of these cries, which echo through the trade publications and technical conferences, is noteworthy. The two major browser developers, Microsoft and Netscape, for years have been turning up the marketing hype for the next versions of their client software. "New features! New technologies! New additions to the W3C standards!" the browser vendors shout. "Buggy code! Incomplete implementations! Inconsistent rendering!" we shout back.

Let's take a look at the historic foundations on which
the browsers were built, the sorry state of affairs for today's
Web developers, and what we can do sort to things out.

Innovation and Legacy

Interoperability is a long tradition throughout the Internet
community. As long as there have been computers talking
to one another, there have been engineers arguing about
the best way to accomplish this.

The unspoken rule worked something like this: A problem would arise ("We need to be able to read e-mail on any
system"), someone would make a proposal ("E-mail headers
should be formatted this way"), and then someone would
hack out code proving it worked. The developers involved
in this conversation would look at the code, discuss the
spec, and then revise it a few times until they were satisfied.
Then someone would type the whole thing up and release it
to the public. Generally, a Request for Comments (RFC)
would be posted on a universally accessible server for anyone to use as a guide for developing interoperable software.

Then came the Web. The outlandish growth we've
experienced over the past few years not only made the standards process difficult, but changed the rules entirely.
Companies developing Web software had to ship new technologies prematurely (in many cases, in order to maintain a
competitive advantage—and fictional stock prices), forgo-
ing the technical analysis that's so important to the development process. Things were suddenly happening in
"Internet Time."

The result of this shift is painfully obvious. Poorly
planned "enhancements" to the defined standards are
impregnated in millions of copies of rushed software. Look
at what happened to Netscape, for example. Responding to
customer demand for visual control in HTML, Netscape
added the <FONT> tag to its Navigator browser. Although the
power and flexibility of Cascading Stylesheets had been
extensively discussed at that time, Netscape snubbed the
standards process and took the easy route, permanently

hurting the Web. Sure, designers could style their text in any of seven predefined sizes, but the semantic meaning of headlines, captions, and subheads were gone forever.

Need more proof? Look at the plethora of ways you can add other media types to your page. Along with the now standard <OBJECT> tag, we also have <EMBED>, <INSERT>, <APP>, <APPLET>, and <IMG>, all of which do the exact same thing.

The frenzied pace of innovation and new-feature development started almost from the beginning. The leap from Netscape's first release to version 2.0 was dramatic, with engineers adding new features (font tags, frames) as fast as they could code them. When Microsoft jumped in with Internet Explorer, the race was on. With each new browser release, Netscape and Microsoft upped the ante. Both scrambled to offer major new features with each version, hoping to prove to the world once and for all which browser was better.

What's the problem? Web developers, Web users, and Web browser marketing managers all have their own definitions of better, which makes for quite a few spectacular mistakes. And, the browser companies have promised to support all their blunders.

Over and over again, the browser companies tell us that they're committed to supporting their content providers and application developers. This, they smugly tell us, is an indication of the high level of support they'll provide for developers who have invested in the browser's cutting-edge technologies. But really it just means that the browser companies are locked into supporting every mistake they've ever made.

Rather than weed out poorly realized technology, the browser companies have resorted to bulky workarounds and add-ons. And the result? We have the bug-ridden, 16-MB-download behemoths we're stuck with today.

After suffering through the side-effects of the browser companies' misguided attempts at "support," developers are now stepping in and asking the most important question: "What should we support?"

Should we just give up?

The reality is that there are as many different views of your site as there are users. Depressing thought, isn't it? (The very notion of having your content, your brand, your very online identity being "interpreted" in millions of ways can strike fear in the most competent creative director or diligent production assistant. So what can we do?

First, it may help to know that you are not alone. In fact, Jupiter Communications recently released a report that surveyed the top 100 commercial Web sites. Jupiter found some disturbing statistics: Nearly two-thirds of these sites were building multiple versions of their Web sites. Those sites spend up to 40 percent of their development resources on building those versions. And very few of the companies polled had any intention of using "new browser technology" on their sites in the near future.

The implications are even worse. How much is it costing the Web industry to make up for the fact that browsers can't get even the most basic standards implemented correctly? How much stifling of innovation is taking place because companies are unwilling to experiment with new technology at the expense of legacy browsers?

It's easy to complain—and trust me, we'll complain in this chapter. It's much more difficult to do something about it. Let's take a look at how to deal with legacy browsers, inconsistent standards support, and the tremendous developmental overhead it takes to deal with the dizzying array of browsers that are out there.

Understanding the Dysfunction

In order to cope with the fractured world of browsers, you'll need an understanding of how broken things really are. We'll start broadly by looking at the industry as a whole, and then narrow the focus to your site in particular. You'll need to dig through a lot of information to make the right choices for your content and your audience—then we'll move from trends to specifics in order to accomplish that.

Here are the questions you will need to ask:

- What browsers are out there?
- What browsers support which tags and technologies?
- How many in my audience are using each browser?

After you are armed with this information, you should be able to make informed choices about your development strategy. In particular, we will be looking at ways to find out which features you should be incorporating in your designs, and how to get the right features for the right browsers.

Why so many?

If you've done any amount of development on the Web, you've probably wished that there was a world with only one browser. "If only I didn't have to deal with all of this complexity. Wouldn't that be wonderful!"

No, actually. It would be the worst possible outcome for our Web.

The Web's very popularity can be attributed in part to its diversity. One of the basic design goals of the nascent World Wide Web was that anyone with any type of computer could access at least some view of your information. To accomplish that, the command-line Internet needed three converging factors in order to succeed: A uniform way to address not only computers connected to the Net, but the individual resources that were on them, a method for transmitting those resources, and a method for displaying them.

The first came in the form of Uniform Resource Locators, known affectionately as URLs. Without them, Net surfers would need to remember not only domain names or IP addresses, but they also would have to decode the applications running on those servers. Today, Web browsers give us a consistent interface to all Net resources, freeing us from the peculiarities of Telnet log-ins and menu navigation.

We won't spend much time on the second necessity. Suffice it to say that the Hypertext Transfer Protocol, more commonly known as HTTP, is saving everybody a lot of grief, despite its many shortcomings. Having all browsers

Before There Were Browsers

Despite its current ubiquity, we didn't always have the Web. We take for granted the instant access to information, the single application with which we consume that information, and the navigational shortcuts that get us there.

But there was a time before search engines, bookmarks, and the "click-here" access that we have today. In fact, it wasn't all that long ago that the only way we could do file transfers was by typing IP numbers into an FTP client, and many resources on the Net were only accessible through something called Telnet.

In the multi-user, command-line world of Unix, gaining access to another machine was done with Telnet. You'd type in the address, log in, and you'd be connected as if you were sitting at that machine. Since there were very few ways to offer interactive information

before the Web, the few services that did exist often made use of Telnet. And if you look hard enough, you can still find a couple of these relics still surviving today.

A good example of how the Net used to work can be found at the University of Michigan's Weather Underground, available by pointing a Telnet client at um-weather.sprl.umich.edu. Try navigating through the hierarchy of weather data. See how long it takes to move up and down the menu system. Marvel at how our Web interfaces work today compared to the terminal-based systems of yesteryear.

Beyond the nostalgia of Telnet applications, you can find basic Information Architectures still in use today with bare-bones interfaces. Things may be easier today, but they are by no means new.

```
SAN FRANCISCO COUNTY-SAN MATEO COUNTY-SANTA CRUZ COUNTY-
400 PM PDT MON APR 10 2000

  TONIGHT...PATCHY FOG AND LOW CLOUDS...OTHERWISE CLEAR.  LOWS
45 TO 50. EVENING SEABREEZE 10 TO 20 MPH.
  TUESDAY...PATCHY MORNING FOG AND LOW CLOUDS...OTHERWISE MOSTLY SUNNY.
HIGHS FROM THE MID 60S AT THE OCEAN NORTH OF SANTA CRUZ TO THE MID 70S
INLAND. NORTHWEST WIND 10 TO 20 MPH ALL DAY AT THE OCEAN NORTH OF
SANTA CRUZ...AFTERNOON SEABREEZE 10 TO 20 MPH ELSEWHERE.
  TUESDAY NIGHT...PATCHY COASTAL LOW CLOUDS AND FOG...OTHERWISE FAIR.
LOWS MID 40S TO LOWER 50S.
  WEDNESDAY...PARTLY CLOUDY.  HIGHS 60S TO LOWER 70S.

       <            TEMPERATURE    / PRECIPITATION
SAN FRANCISCO        46  65  48  60 /  00  00  00  00
SFO AIRPORT          48  68  50  64 /  00  00  00  00
REDWOOD CITY         46  71  48  67 /  00  00  00  00
SANTA CRUZ           46  72  48  69 /  00  00  00  00

  EXTENDED FORECAST...
  THURSDAY THROUGH SATURDAY...VARIABLE CLOUDINESS AND COOLER WITH A
CHANCE OF SHOWERS.  LOWS MID 40S TO LOWER 50S.  HIGHS UPPER 50S TO
MID 60S.
    Press Return to continue, M to return to menu, X to exit:
```

The University of Michigan's Weather Underground system is still available via a tel-net interface—interesting if only from a historical perspective.

and all servers speak the same language behind the scenes may very well be the most important reason we're all using the Web today.

But what concerns us here is the final converging factor: A standard way of displaying Web resources.

The Hypertext Markup Language was designed to be simple, forgivable, and viewable on any type of computer. And that was supposed to mean everyone—from dumb terminals wired to mainframes to the fastest, highest-resolution, multimedia-capable desktop machines and even wireless cell phones.

While this may sound like an admirable goal, the harsh reality played out significantly differently. Browsers got popular in a hurry, and those making browsers responded to their customers' demands by adding tags and technologies as quickly as they could. Soon, the world was filled with hundreds of browsers—as was the intent of HTML all along—but those browsers were rendering content in hundreds of different ways. And while the Web should scale to accommodate any surfer, the fact is that most document authors want to maintain at least a modicum of control over the appearance of their documents. Today, we're left with a diverse yet fractioned medium on which to base our products. With so little consistency across browsers, you may find yourself ready to throw up your hands and surrender. Why bother?

I'll tell you why. The solution isn't all that hard.

Understanding the Problem

As I mentioned before, there is a confusing variety of browsers, versions, computer platforms, and other variables that conspire to make your site look broken somewhere, somehow. Factor into all of that the reality that no browser is bug free. You may actually be *doing the right thing* and still your site looks broken. What to do?

You could bury your head in the sand and simply build sites that make use of the tiny subset of tags that work in all browsers. If you're comfortable with `<H1>` and `<P>`, then you're pretty much set. You're site will look remarkably like an academic paper, but it will work everywhere and you'll be able to sleep at night knowing your site is rendering with perfection across the Web.

Most of us, however, would rather build a site that communicates visually as well as structurally—a site with an appropriate amount of branding and identity. This means taking chances—calculated risks, actually—with the tags and technologies you incorporate into your design. It also means much more work for you, since you'll not only have to build multiple versions of your site to ensure compatibility, you'll need to discover *who* needs to get *what* too.

Don't worry, it's not as hard as it sounds. Quite a few people have done this before, and many of them now share the tools they've developed to help keep track of all of this. Let's dig in.

We're going to start by looking very broadly at the industry as a whole, both by analyzing a bit of historical data, and then seeing how that data is at work in today's browser statistics. That should give us a good idea how many people are using which browsers across the Web. More importantly, though, is what *your* audience is using on *your* site. To get at that information, we'll dig into some lightweight server-log analyses tools. With that knowledge in mind, you can start to make decisions about which features you should incorporate into your Web site. Finally, we'll dig into how to serve multiple interfaces to multiple browsers, allowing you to explore some cutting-edge technology while still providing a usable experience for your entire audience.

Scouting the Industry

Brace yourself: I'm going to throw a very disturbing statistic at you. At the time of this writing, the Yahoo category "Home > Computers and Internet > Software > Internet > World Wide Web > Browsers" contained 148 distinct and separate browser listings. And that doesn't take into account the scores of versions each individual browser may have. Netscape's Navigator, for example, has released browsers both for 16-bit and 32-bit machines running Windows, the Macintosh, and a variety of Unix flavors. For each one of those platforms, there were dozens of versions over the years, from early betas to the differences between "standard" and "gold" releases. And it doesn't stop at "traditional" releases for mainstream desktop computers. People have developed browsers for the handheld Palm Pilot crowd, Braille readers for seeing impaired users, clients for those Internet terminals in airports. Have you ever seen a gas pump with a monitor on it as you're filling your car? Yup, there's an old version of Mosaic for it. It's a fractal problem: The more browsers you look for, the more you'll find.

Thankfully, we can pare that number down a bit. Our basic strategy, which we'll get to in more detail later, is to divide and conquer. We'll determine how many versions of our sites we can manage, and create "buckets" into which we can group particular browsers. In its easiest form, our strategy will call for a high-end version and a low-end version, with the thousands of browser combinations neatly organized into those two buckets, with the appropriate interfaces being served to each.

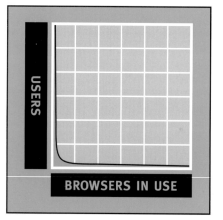

Who's surfing with what? The fact is, most people use the most popular browsers, but the trail of browsers in use is incredibly long.

So, back to the task at hand—getting a handle on the vast number of different browsers. It's probably not a surprise that, while there are lots of browsers, only a few are being used by a substantial percentage of your audience. In fact, browser usage follows a Zipf curve pretty closely. A Zipf curve merely shows data that cluster around a few popular choices, even though the data being displayed have many, many possible selections.

What does this mean for your site? Well, despite the fact that industry browser reports show browsers for the Commodore Amiga and early beta versions of Navigator in circulation, the reality is that they make up an infinitely small percentage of total page views and user sessions across the Web. So you should ignore them, right? Wrong. Our pages should accommodate everyone, but we'll get to that.

What are most people using then? It's safe to say that they are, in general, sticking to either Netscape Navigator or Microsoft's Internet Explorer. Let's look at how the numbers are stacking up at the moment. On the popular developer site BrowserWatch (www.browserwatch.com), the site's caretaker Dave Garaffa maintains a page detailing the browsers that visit his site. As of this writing, Internet Explorer was being used by 62.6 percent of his audience, while Netscape was holding with 21.7 percent. Thus, over 86 percent of this particular audience is using one of the two leading commercial browsers, with the remaining 14 percent trailing off across dozens of others.

But remember, the BrowserWatch audience is skewed towards developers who are looking for information on browsers—a very specific group of people who may have significantly different tastes in software adoption than your audience. To get an even more accurate picture of the rest of the Web, we can look to The Counter (www.thecounter.com). This site offers a typical free service: The page counter

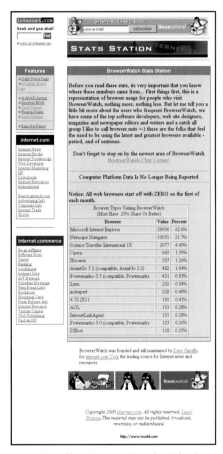

Dave Garaffa's BrowserWatch Web site not only collects browser usage statistics, but is a good source of up-to-the-minute industry news on what Web client software is being released.

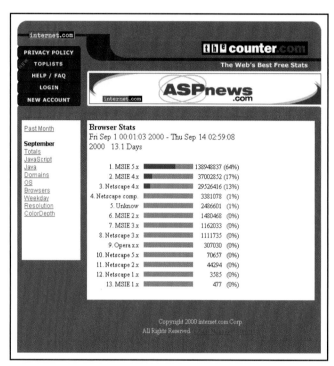

Free statistics, offered for the good of the industry—and the associated publicity, of course. The Counter shows just how dramatically audience plays into browser usage numbers. Here, with a sample from the broader Web, we see Microsoft in the clear majority of Web clients.

popular with so many amateur Web sites that are willing to display to the world how much (or, more often, how little) traffic they are getting. You've probably seen the little images that look like odometers proclaiming "This site has been visited 0012 times!" What The Counter does differently, though, is keep track of who is viewing what across the millions of counters they've distributed. They then aggregate that information and offer it publicly as a free service to Web developers. Their statistics show even finer grain detail than BrowserWatch. As of this writing, Microsoft is leading. If we add up the IE numbers, we see that the Microsoft browser is being used by a whopping 81 percent of the browsing public—a radically different number than BrowserWatch, and probably a more accurate snapshot of what is really happening on the Web. I'm showing you this discrepancy for a reason, though. Your site can also be dramatically different from industry numbers—your audience is your own.

We're now equipped to follow the industry numbers for browser usage. But gathering data on Web-wide usage is only half the equation—we also need to look at new versions, old versions, and the rate at which browsers are upgraded. There are few things more tantalizing to a Web designer than the promise of new browsers and new features. And there is nothing more disheartening than the inability to use them. Why? If your users don't have supporting browsers, then nobody will see what you've done. So again we ask, "What to do?"

Old Browsers Never Die

Never has a piece of software seen such rapid adoption as the first version of the free Netscape browser. It was Fall of 1994 and the Web was young. The dominant browser at the time, was a graduate project from the National Center for Super Computing Applications at the University of Illinois, Champaign-Urbana. "NCSA Mosaic" was exceedingly popular, since it was the first browser capable of showing inline images. But when Netscape Communication's "Mozilla" browser hit the Web, everything changed. Nearly overnight, the new browser commandeered a tremendous user base. Everyone who was online at the time, it seemed, switched to Netscape.

That overnight conversion didn't quite keep up, however. New versions of the browser were released almost monthly. It seemed like a full-time job just downloading and installing new versions of the Netscape software. Then, a year or so later, Microsoft joined the fray with its Internet Explorer browser. They, too, iterated with gusto. A couple of years into the so-called "browser wars" and it was impossible to keep the myriad of versions straight.

To gain any sort of historical perspective on browser adoption by a general Web audience, we need to look at *years* rather than *versions*. The chart below shows how the statistics have played out over the last 5 years. Note that these are aggregate numbers based on features roughly assigned to version numbers—that is, Netscape's second version was roughly equivalent to Microsoft's. Netscape 4 and IE4, likewise, held similarly equal feature sets (with wildly divergent quality, but more on that later). So it's fair to look at how the numbered versions waxed and waned in usage throughout the last decade.

As we've seen, the popularity of the first version of Netscape's browser back in 1994 skyrocketed into the 90th

Browser Upgrades Through the Years

As new versions of browsers are released, users upgrade rapidly. But they don't all upgrade, as this chart shows. On the left is the percentage of Web users surfing with any particular browser. Along the bottom, the progres-sion of time. See how each previous version of a browser trails on through the years? Since not every one can or will upgrade, no browser will ever fully eclipse the others. The result is a frac-tured user base.

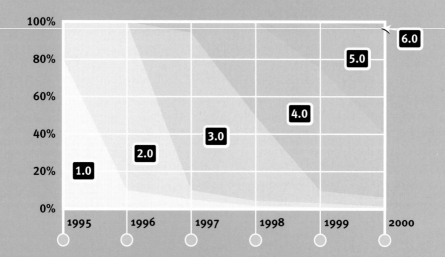

percentile nearly overnight. But the same certainly didn't happen with the second version. What we saw instead was a steady 5 to 10 percent attrition to new versions per month. So when a new, major release of the browser hit, it could take nearly 16 months for the old version to finally go away. Except that it didn't. Let me explain.

Not everyone, unfortunately, has a choice when it comes to browsers. While most of the readers of a book like this install and delete new software with impunity, there are scores of users who don't have the same desktop freedom. Many users are at the whim of their "technology managers." These are the folks who do the remarkable job of keeping corporate information systems running efficiently. Thus, they have the power to decide which software will be rolled out across their networks, and when. So, just because Netscape or Microsoft touts the features of its brand new browser doesn't mean these managers will upgrade. And when these folks are making decisions for tens of thousands of desktops in the world's largest corporations, the numbers can drag on for what seems like an eternity.

The slow upgrade effect was compounded by the 1997 release of the version 4 browsers. The battle for Web supremacy was raging between Netscape and Microsoft. The respective companies squared off on the desktop: Both proclaimed that their browsers would support nearly complete integration into your computer's operating system. When they both finally released their shiny new browsers, the result was a resounding thud from users across the Web. Suddenly upgrading your simple Web browser meant upgrading your entire operating system—something most people (and almost all companies) don't take very lightly at all. The conversion rate slowed down considerably; so slow that we've only recently caught up.

And don't forget home users. Without the support of a corporate helpdesk, many home users are rightly hesitant to mess with a tenuous computer system that happens to be working just fine right now, thank you very much. We often make the false assumption that our amazing, dynamic inter-

As I mentioned, this chunk of identification gets stamped into your server log and is waiting patiently to be of use in your research. Most log analyses tools will give you some measure of control over how this is done, usually how specific you'd like your report to be. You can generally get just browser numbers, just version numbers, or other levels of detail.

The Numbers Game

There are a couple of ways to get at this information, depending on whether you actually can access your server logs. At issue is how much control you have over your server. If you're the one managing the systems that serve your Web pages, then getting those logs is a relatively straight-forward task. If, however, your servers are managed by someone else in your organization, or—as is more frequently the case—your site is hosted by a service provider or one of the Web's many free homepage services, then you'll need to use a different method for digging into the wonderful world of server statistics. Regardless, the process isn't all that difficult. Let's look at the different approaches.

We'll start with those of you fortunate enough to have access to your own server logs. For you, the options are more varied and powerful. First, you'll have to decide whether to install a log analysis tool that looks directly at your data, or to pull the logs over to a desktop machine and do the analysis there. Products like Hit List from Accrue Software, Inc. or the variety of tools available from WebTrends Corporation are examples of tools that look directly at your data. They can be installed on servers and generate reports as often as you like, with near infinite customization options. You can, for example, use tools like this to create custom reports on just which browsers are being used and by whom, and then have that report run automatically and e-mail the results to you every Monday morning. Intelligence delivered to your inbox, as it were.

If you can't install the software on a server, opt for a free log-parsing tool like Analog, or The Webalizer (which is

Running Reports with Analog

It may feel like a relic, but the log-analysis tool Analog is a powerful—and free—tool for quickly extracting valuable information from the ocean of data in your server logs.

You can pick up a copy of Analog at `http://www.analog.cx/`. Once you've downloaded and installed it, there are a few simple steps to get it working. Open the configuration file in a text editor. (Sorry, you'll have to do without such comforts as a GUI with preferences in dialog boxes.) The settings contained within allow you a tremendous amount of customization, but we're going to focus on browser statistics for now. Tell the application where your server logs are, either on the network or where you copied them over to your local machine. Then, change the browser report setting to your preference: either detailed or a quick overview. To do this, you'll need to set the BROWSER or FULLBROWSER directives to ON in the `analog.cfg` file. Now set Analog to work, sit back, and wait for the goodies.

Your report will end up in Analog's default folder (unless you changed that when you configured) as `report.html`. It should be in HTML format, which means you can simply open it up in a browser and have a look. Below all the traffic reports, you'll find the exact number of browsers in use on your site. You can now start to make decisions about your target audience and what technologies you can safely use on your site.

Set up a little scheduler to run the report with new data regularly, and you'll have all the information you'll need with a minimal amount of effort—something we all strive for.

Analog reports may not be pretty to look at, but they do contain valuable information. The report here shows an overview of browser usage.

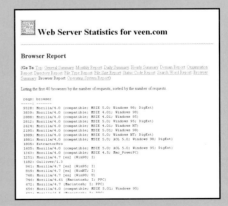

Traffic reports, right in your browser. This detail of browser version usage can be easily dumped into a spreadsheet application for manipulation and chart generation.

available from `www.mrunix.net/webalizer`). These are simple software packages that you can use on your personal computer. Once installed, you'll need to get access to your server logs—either point the tool at them on a server somewhere, or download the actual data to your machine and set the software running. Again, the choices for reporting are almost overwhelming.

Finally, if you don't have access to your logs, don't worry. You can still find out who is using your site and with what client—but you won't have the flexibility or customization options of dedicated software packages. There are a number of free services on the Web that can track your site's usage for you. You'll generally need to put some sort of "counter" or other bit of code on each page you want watched. Then, each time your page is loaded, a slew of data will be transmitted via HTTP headers to the third-party site, which will track and store that information for you. Later, you can visit the service and see your statistics (and usually a few ad banners).

The disadvantages to these services are numerous. You'll need to fit their "branding button" into your interface. Their code may slow down your page. You'll have to trust the service with potentially sensitive traffic information. But they are free, and often they are the only alternative if you don't have a dedicated server. We've already looked at TheCounter.com's global statistics. This is how they get this data, and it also is how you can add the tracking service to your site. Hitbox.com is another option, with even more detailed information. A search for "Web counters" on any search engine will turn up dozens more.

Use Your Numbers

Once you've got the data from your Web site, it's time to put it to use. But before you do, it's important to understand just what that information means. You might be surprised to find your numbers don't match the rest of the Web. Earlier in this chapter, I demonstrated that effect with the BrowserWatch statistics. Their site is aimed at developers who make different browser decisions than those of the general population. Your site may have a similar audience skew, and a first look at your statistics may confirm this.

You might also learn something else: Your site's design is a filter. It may seem like an obvious fact—that the technologies you choose will necessarily limit the audience you attract—but it's an important lesson to keep in mind. For example, if you make use of technologies only supported in later versions of popular browsers (think dynamic positioning with CSS and JavaScript), and don't bother creating an alternative interface for users with browsers that don't support these features, your statistics will be skewed toward the high end. For this reason, it's important to generate two different traffic reports with your log analysis tool: One that shows users per browser, and one that shows page views per browser. And, the difference may be dramatic. A site optimized for high-end browsers may get 10 times more traffic with those browsers, even if the number of users is comparable.

So great, you've got your numbers together and can see a fairly clear picture of who is using your site. Now, you need to make a big decision: What browser tags and technologies are you going to use? To make these choices, you'll need to know which browsers and versions support which features, and then map that to the number of users for each that you have. Then, you can make a clear choice, and begin to formulate a strategy for targeting each group.

We'll start with tags. As HTML developed, it fractured. Some browsers supported tags from published W3C specifications, others developed their own proprietary tags. As the browsers iterated, they began to adopt new tags at different rates. Thus, a particular 3.0 client may not support a feature in a competing 2.0 version. Keeping this all straight is, frankly, a nightmare.

Thankfully, there's help. A number of Web sites have been created to document this fractured development. One of the best (if you can ignore the awkward interface) is Index Dot HTML, at `www.blooberry.com/indexdot/`. The charts on this site show each tag and attribute, and how they have been supported over time. There are columns that show when a particular tag was first published in a W3C specification, and when it was implemented in the browsers with the largest user base. The detail is phenomenal. For example, you can check which browsers support not only frames, but each attribute available to that tag, such as frameborder, bordercolor, marginwidth, and on and on. Truly an invaluable resource for making design decisions.

Index Dot HTML only deals with tags and attributes, however. For a broader perspective, try Webmonkey's BrowserKit at `www.webmonkey.com/browserkit/`. This page

Alternative Browsers

It's true that the browser universe has collapsed into two primary competitors: Internet Explorer and Netscape. Yet, things aren't always so clean cut. For example, the world's largest provider of Internet service, America Online, uses a special version of Internet Explorer with a feature set that doesn't quite match that of the one released publicly by Microsoft. Add to that the folks surfing your site through their televisions. You didn't think you'd get off that easily, did you?

Thankfully, these specific browsers have plenty of documentation to support them (and you). America Online, for example, has compiled a staggering amount of information for developers, available online at `webmaster.info.aol.com/`. Here, you'll find extensive charts of which features are supported in each version of the AOL browsers, and just how many in

its audience have upgraded. You can also find documentation on what AOL does to compress images, how to work around the caching scheme they use, and more. Regardless of whether you target AOL users, it pays to spend some time reading through this site.

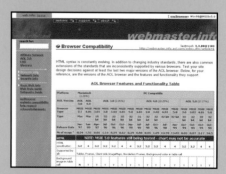

Excruciatingly detailed information on the AOL browser features and usage at the America Online Webmaster Info site.

documents things like JavaScript, Cascading Stylesheets, and XML support across the major browsers, and distinguishes across platforms as well. Formatted in a neat table, you can simply look down a column and see if there are enough boxes filled in for your level of support. Again, this is an easy decision-making process.

Other technologies have whole sites dedicated to them. Cascading Stylesheets, for example, have great potential but an unbelievably spotty implementation in current browsers. To track the massive specification across all versions of browsers, the WebReview site has created a special section at `style.webreview.com`. By now, you'll notice the familiar rows and columns of a support table popular with

Worried about how your site works with the WebTV box? You should be. While the usage numbers for WebTV aren't all that high, they are growing and could be a significant portion of your audience someday. Like AOL, there is plenty of useful information on the WebTV site at `developer.webtv.net/`, including an emulator for their browser. You can download and install this application and run the WebTV client on your desktop machine. Surfing through your pages undoubtedly will be an enlightening experience, considering how many liberties the browser takes with table layout and typography.

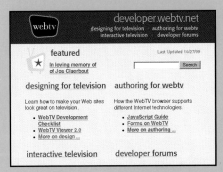

The WebTV developer site offers tutorials for television Web design, plus an emulator to test your site.

Curious what your site looks like on TV? Download the WebTV emulator and have at it. And yes, you can even use the remote control to experience the full user experience.

sites like this. WebReview gets into very specific detail in their table, matching up not only implemented features of the specification, but making notes of bugs and weird behavior in the browsers.

Choose a Strategy

By now, you have a firm understanding of the research tools available to you. We've looked at the historical trends in browser adoption. We've analyzed the industry trends for browser usage and compared them to a number specific to our sites. We've mapped those numbers to the technologies we wish to incorporate into our sites. Now, we need to develop a strategy for creating Web interfaces that accommodate the audience and technologies we've decided to target.

To develop a methodology for developing our sites, we're going to examine three different strategies for dealing with multiple browsers:

- Don't ask, don't tell
- Browser-specific exploitations
- Conditional serving

None of these strategies can exist in a vacuum. As we dig into each, we'll look at how they overlap.

Don't Ask, Don't Tell

The easiest possible strategy is really no strategy at all. Rather, you could ignore the problem all together and create the simplest possible page that works in all browsers. Well, you *could* do that, but where do you draw the line?

One solution is to employ only the simple code the browsers managed to get right. This includes basic HTML (probably somewhere in the neighborhood of version 3.2), with things like tables, frames, font tags, and maybe even a plug-in or applet. These pages were written by the developers, authors, and designers who can't afford the resources needed to play the cutting-edge tech game. They've staked out a simple plot of Web frontier and are happily coexisting with technology from three browser versions ago. Developers in this first group build the majority of today's Web sites.

Many of the research tools we talked about earlier in this chapter can feed the sense of security that comes from embracing a "don't ask, don't tell" strategy. We're not going to bother with advanced (and typically buggy) technologies. We're not going to worry about the complexity of backend scripting engines publishing multiple versions of our sites. Rather, we'll take the simple route and, by using tools that show us compatibility like Index Dot HTML, define a very narrow set of tags and technologies. Sites like these probably won't win awards for innovation, but they will satisfy the needs of the largest group of users. And isn't that the point after all?

HTML was designed to "degrade gracefully"—meaning every version of the HTML specification published by the W3C was guaranteed not to break previous versions. Thus, if a browser doesn't understand a particular new tag, it is required to just keep going as best it can. That way, you can use things like the `<IMG>` tag to drop images into your pages, but satisfy anybody by including the `"ALT="` attribute with rich textual descriptions. HTML is filled with fallbacks like this, and it pays to exploit them not only with the simple strategy we're describing here, but even as an ultimate safety net on more complex multi-browser strategies.

Look at the multiple levels of content support in this example:

```
<object src="cat.mov">
  <img "cat.jpg" alt="My Cat Alex">
</object>
```

Here, we have an embedded QuickTime movie of my wonderful cat, Alex. But for users without the ability to display inline digital video, I've included a still shot as a JPEG image. Older browsers, not understanding the `<object>` tag, will safely ignore it and display the image instead. No graphics displaying? The alt text degrades even further for search engines or users of devices that read Web pages to them. And on and on. Degradability is the best way to ensure compatibility.

Browser-Specific Exploitations

On the other end of the spectrum are the experimenters. These are the "early adopters," the Type-A personalities who enjoy exploring the cutting-edge of browser capabilities. These developers jump at the chance to play with the new toys, constantly reinventing what is possible on the Web, and defining what's next for the rest of us. The sites they create typically don't scale back to encompass the entire Web audience and are easy to spot. Just look for buttons and warnings proclaiming "best when viewed with..."

We don't need to talk again about the strengths and weaknesses of a strategy that exploits cutting-edge technology. Suffice it to say, though, that making the choice to abandon users of older browsers is not just an interface call, it's a business decision as well.

Conditional Serving

The third group consists of the rest of us, people forced to deal with the reality of publishing on the Web today. Whether developing commercially or as hobbyists, we don't want to turn away a significant percentage of our audience simply because they won't (or can't) upgrade their browsers as quickly as we'd like. But still, we love the Web, we love what's possible, and we want to move in the direction set by the experimenters I described above. The solution? Multiple versions of content for multiple versions of browsers. Using code running on our servers or written as scripts embedded in our pages, we sniff out the browser versions and platform choices of our users and serve handcrafted bits and pieces of our pages.

After doing this multiple-personality work for years, we know that it's nearly impossible to keep up with the myriad of browser and platform combinations. To make things easier on ourselves, many of us define the high-end and low-end, and then clump browsers into their respective bins. Slowly, over time, the collective Web audience upgrades, and new features trickle down from high to low. For example, in the early days of the Web, I was developing versions of pages for browsers that didn't support tables. I no longer do this. As browser adoption shifts in new ways, we'll continue to adjust who gets what. Netscape's Cascading Stylesheets implementation was so bad in Navigator 4.0 that relegating that browser to the low-end bucket has saved me an infinite amount of grief. It took a long time for enough of my audience to shift over to Microsoft's browser before I felt comfortable doing that, however. By now, you should know where to go for research on your particular audience's preference for browsers. The same thing will happen in months and years to come with the technologies that are emerging today. And you'll need to continue to keep track.

Of course, this is bound directly to developer frustration. While the Web appears to be speeding along at an unbelievable clip, most of us are forced to wait for the features we crave to be embraced by a wide enough audience. And every day that ticks by with nonstandard browser hacks and inconsistent implementations means a decrease in the adoption rate. And more waiting.

So how do we go about doing this multiple-version switching? There are two ways: the browser or the server. Let's look at both.

Client-Side Conditional Serving

Regardless of the path you take to conditional serving, the process will require some sort of conditional logic. Some bit of code will have to take a look at the User Agent String, parse it into the discernable parts, and make a decision as to which chunk of code or alternate page design the browser should get. You need to decide whether or not those scripts will live and run on your server, or will be embedded in your page's source code to be executed by the user's browser. There are benefits and drawbacks to both.

Sending JavaScript with your HTML to do the browser detection and code switching can be very simple. The example on the following page shows just how easy it is to use an HTML editor (in this case Macromedia Dreamweaver) to quickly make the decision as to what code will be going to what browser. Enter a couple of URLs, select a few options, click OK, and you're finished.

Even if you're more comfortable writing things by hand, the process is easy. Your code will simply check the browser's

Checking Browsers with Dreamweaver

Using an HTML editor such as Macromedia's Dreamweaver can make even complicated tasks a matter of point and click. To include a rudimentary browser negotiation script in your pages, for example, takes only a couple of simple steps. First, select the "Check Browser" option from the pulldown menu on the Behaviors pallet. Then, simply use the resulting dialog box to choose which browser should get which version of your interface.

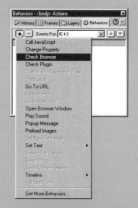

In this example, I've created a high-end page designed for Internet Explorer 4.0 and higher, and a low-end version for every other browser. To accomplish this, I simply enter the alternate URL for the low-end page, and tell the script which browsers should be redirected there. Other HTML editors like Adobe's GoLive have similar functionality.

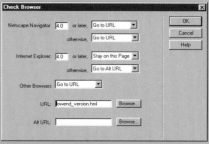

Adding a conditional browser script to your site can be as easy as selecting a Behavior in Dreamweaver.

identity, then switch (in the following example) among multiple stylesheets.

```
<SCRIPT> <!--
// Windows IE 4 or later...
  if ((document.images) &&
  (navigator.appName != "Netscape") &&
  (navigator.appVersion.indexOf('Mac') == -1))
    {
    document.writeln("<link rel=\"stylesheet\"
    type=\"text/css\" href=\"ie.css\">")
    };

// Navigator 4...
  if ((navigator.appName == "Netscape") &&
  (parseInt(navigator.appVersion) == 4))
    {
    document.writeln("<link rel=\"stylesheet\"
    type=\"text/css\" href=\"nav.css\">")
    };
-->
</SCRIPT>
```

The code merely checks for the appropriate "`appName`" and "`appVersion`," and then adds a `<LINK>` tag to the document pointing to the correct stylesheet.

Things aren't quite this foolproof, however. There have been a number of security issues with browser scripting that have caused a number of users to disable that browser feature. With JavaScript crippled, none of the conditionalizing we've just explored will work at all. And your users most likely won't see any errors. Instead, they'll see your pages without the style information, or with broken features unsupported in their browsers. Depending on the complexity of your pages, this could render your pages as attractive as a physics paper, or a confusing spew of unintelligible code.

One final drawback to the simplicity of client-side code: performance. If you're providing two versions of your pages, with the switch happening in JavaScript, some of your users most likely will end up downloading both pages, but only displaying the one intended for them. Users of low-end browsers, for example, would come to your page, download the code, execute the code, then get redirected to the page designed for them. Thus, not only do they download more bytes, but they also have to take the time to bounce over to the right page. Not the best user experience.

The better solution is most likely found on your server.

Server-Side Conditional Serving

Rather than risk broken pages and slower user experiences, we should look to server technology for answers. The ideal situation would have the server detecting what browser a user has, and then sending just the correct code for that configuration. This way, regardless of what the user's security settings are, you can be assured that they're seeing the interface you intended.

There are a wide variety of server-based scripting systems. You may have heard of Microsoft's Active Server Pages, or Allaire's Cold Fusion, or even PHP or Embedded Perl. These are all methods of executing code on your server whenever a user asks for a page. We won't get into the details of that now; we'll talk more about dynamic publishing in Chapter Eight, "Object-Oriented Publishing."

Conceptually, what you'll be doing on the server is nearly identical to what you would have done on in the browser. In most cases, a few lines of code will access the User Agent String and parse it (in some languages this is done automatically—you just ask for the result). Then, you can make your interface decisions by writing conditional logic that switches between different chunks of your code.

Beyond the assurance that the scripts will run, you can also get much more sophisticated in how you serve different pieces of HTML. Here are a few different architectures for server-based browser detection:

- **Many versions of the page**: You can create a tiny script that redirects users from the URL they followed to the appropriate version of the page for them. Very simple code, but now you'll have multiple versions of your content.
- **One version, many switches**: This is a very popular way to make your pages work in many browsers. Just write one version of the page, then add little if…then statements for each piece that's broken in a particular browser.
- **"Forking"**: A more complicated version of the example above. Think of each part of your page as a separate chunk. Each chunk of the page gets wrapped in browser-specific code, gets assembled into one big page, and then sent to the browser. This separates the content from the presentation and makes both more manageable, but it takes a lot of planning up front.

A brighter future?

If this seems like an awful lot of work, you're right. It is. Developers and designers are spending countless hours reworking their pages or, worse, giving up entirely and pushing out lowest-common-denominator code, stifling innovation that could benefit the user experience on their sites. Can't something be done? The Internet was running on standards for a couple of decades before the Web. Isn't anybody doing anything about this?

Yes. The World Wide Web Consortium.

But first, a bit more history. There's been a longstanding (and SGML-based) utopian ideal of completely separating the presentation of electronic content from its semantic meaning. I've preached the importance of that in these pages, and it remains the foundation of many Web technologies.

What does this have to do with the standards problem? In a nutshell, Web developers and designers expect their content to behave in a consistent way. The Hypertext

Markup Language, however, was never designed to be displayed in a standard way—a very important premise to remember. From the beginning, HTML was created to react and adapt to whatever computer, display, or device that was reading it, which means an `<H1>` element on my computer could look completely different from an `<H1>` element on your PalmPilot.

Well, that was the ideal. The reality was that nearly everyone surfing the Web has similar computer systems running comparable browsers. The result? A de facto standard for the visual display of HTML. When we mark our text with tags, we expect those tags to look the same everywhere—even though that rubs against the very grain of HTML. When I lay out a page of text, there had better be the same amount of space between my paragraphs on both browsers. If not, one seems broken. Who wants that?

The bigger problem, of course, is that this informal rendering standard doesn't scale. More tags kept getting added to HTML, and with them an implied rendering. At this point, it's just too difficult to keep up with all the little quirks. `<p>` tags render differently when inside `<li>` tags. There's more space in table cells if the `</TD>` is on a different line than the content. What a headache.

The Browser Solution

But even if the W3C were to develop a perfect standard for presentation-free HTML and a robust style language, the browser companies would still have to implement it. And that's been a problem from day one, if today's buggy and incomplete browsers are any indication.

Netscape and Microsoft (and everyone competing with them) have some work to do. Most importantly, they have to shift from being end-user software companies and morph into producers of consumer goods.

In his latest book *The Invisible Computer*, Donald Norman digs into some of the fundamental problems with the computer industry. He starts with an interesting question: How many of you have bought a watch recently because it tells better time than the rest? Nobody has, of course. All watches keep time accurately within a second or two a day. Rather, you choose a timepiece based on other factors: style, alarm features, time zone translations, and so on. The Web's inventor said it best:

> *Anyone who slaps a 'this page is best viewed with Browser X' label on a Web page appears to be yearning for the bad old days, before the Web, when you had very little chance of reading a document written on another computer, another word processor, or another network.*
>
> –Tim Berners-Lee
> *Technology Review*, July 1996.

This same sort of default assumption needs to apply to our browsers. We need to get to the point where the display of Web content is taken for granted, with all browsers supporting all tags, style, and scripting at the same level. Just like your watch keeps time, your telephone calls other phones, and your stereo accepts all compact discs. There needs to be no such thing as "best viewed with...." Instead, browser companies must distinguish their products with other features: Speed, user interface, desktop integration, or any of the other decision points that consumers use before making a purchase.

Until then, we'll continue to struggle with an incompatible Web.

Chapter Six

Speed

The Web is an amazing expression of hypermedia, personal storytelling, and the interconnectedness of everyone on the planet. It's also an incredibly difficult place to make a living.

How fast is your Web site? Do pages load in 5 seconds? Ten? Do you even know?

It doesn't matter how cool and exciting that animated logo is, no matter how

important it is to get that picture of the CEO on the front page, you'll lose more

traffic to the principle of speed than any other. In this chapter, we'll look at ways

to make our sites as fast as they possibly can be. We'll start by looking at just how

fast your pages need to be, using techniques such as the Stopwatch Analysis, to

peeking behind the scenes of your competition to see where they stand. Then,

it's time to get your site into shape by scrubbing every last byte from your code,

and—borrowing from the magician's practice of sleight of hand—dealing with

the perception of speed versus the reality of slow-loading pages.

If there's one thing you can count on in the Web industry, it's the fictional future. Ask any developer or designer what's coming next, and you're bound to hear, "Well, as soon as we have faster bandwidth…."

We've heard over and over again—from users, from pundits, and from the scientists in our usability labs—the number one plague facing today's Web is *speed*. Users are frustrated, especially those new to the surfing experience who have absolutely no patience for cell after cell of our tables pouring painfully into their browsers. If only the Web were faster.

Broadband is promised in press release after press release. So-and-so has just done a US$20 billion deal to provide high-speed access to four homes in suburban Atlanta. Cable modems are being rolled out as we speak. Bandwidth! Bandwidth! Bandwidth!

Fact is, we've been saying the same thing over and over again for the 5 years there has been a commercial Web. And, we'll probably keep saying this for at least 5 more years.

Connecting with the Past

You probably already know about Moore's law, in which computer technology gets twice as fast and half as expensive in this industry every 18 months. And while that certainly has held true for hardware, the same can't be said for connection speeds. In fact, the Web got a lot slower before it started speeding up. Way back in 1994, the audience coming to HotWired.com was split into three groups: a third on 14.4kbps modems, a third in the 56kbps line/ISDN group, and another third coming to us on big industrial T1s. Naturally, we assumed that users would consistently migrate to faster and faster connections as more companies upgraded their infrastructure, users ditched their modems, and broadband became ubiquitous in homes around the world. After all, if our computers were shooting from 100 megahertz to 1 gigahertz in just a few years, think what connection speed would do.

But that's not what happened. While many did, in fact, upgrade to faster modems and dedicated connections, an unexpected thing happened: the Internet got very, very popular. And this popularity didn't strike equally across our user base. Rather, millions and millions of people came online at once, and all with low-end modems. When America Online, for example, upgraded their service to include a gateway to the Internet in 1995, they opened a floodgate of users who had no other option than 14.4kbps modem connections. Suddenly, the numbers shifted. Now, the vast majority of users came to our sites with much slower connections. Our experimentation into digital video over the Web suddenly became far less interesting. In fact, almost all of our attention shifted to creating new Web interfaces that were as small and as fast as they possibly could be.

The last couple of years have been better, sure, but in an evolutionary sense. Modem users have more than doubled their speeds on average, from 14.4kbps to 33.6kbps. But that is it for modems. The technology has run its course. The current maximum speed of 56kbps is quite literally the limit; they simply cannot be made to go faster. And 56kbps isn't quite the reality at that. Due to FCC regulations, these modems can only really achieve a maximum speed of 53kbps, and most homes have fairly bad wiring, forcing the upper limit at a paltry 40kbps. And broadband? Home usage as of this writing is only about 6 percent in North America. We certainly haven't had any paradigm-shattering leaps en mass to cable modems, DSL, or any other fat-pipe solution to the home.

Want to know a dirty little secret? I've been surfing for the past few years on a T3 digital leased line from my offices. That's about as much bandwidth as anybody could possibly need. Pages load as if from my hard drive. Software updates zip down seemingly instantly. MP3 files stream in real-time. And you know what? I never want the Web sites I visit to get any slower. Ever.

Think about using applications on your computer. If you have a reasonably fast desktop machine, most functions happen in less than a second. Click "Print" and a dialog box comes up before you notice. Drag a file from one place to another and the icons on the screen respond in real time.

We take this type of interaction for granted. That's how computers are supposed to work—they respond to our commands. If they don't, something feels wrong. Did I crash? Do I need more memory? Why isn't anything happening?

The Web is a completely different experience, however. Sites—even those offering Web-based applications—creep along like an ancient mainframe. But what if using a search

Express Checkout—E-commerce Style

There has been no shortage of hype and excitement over the possibility of redefining retail shopping through e-commerce. The reality, however, has been a strange mix of corporate efficiency and user dissatisfaction. Why? It is true that many e-commerce sites have been created by relatively new companies. Order tracking and fulfillment is difficult to get right.

Customer support people are hard to find and train. Warehouse management is an acquired skill. And all of those attributes show up in surveys of Web users who have shopped online. But as the chart below shows, the top grievance of the majority of shoppers can be traced directly back to page design. If a site is slow, shoppers give up.

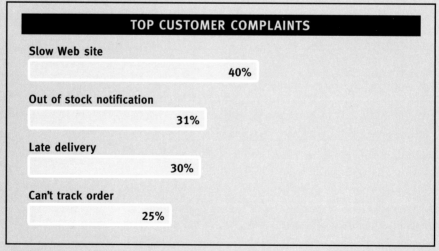

TOP CUSTOMER COMPLAINTS

Slow Web site
40%

Out of stock notification
31%

Late delivery
30%

Can't track order
25%

This data, from a May 2000 report published by biztalk.com, measures customer satisfaction with online shopping during the previous year's holiday season. Forty percent of all shoppers were frustrated by long downloads while trying to complete their purchases. In a very plain sense, bandwidth equals money.

engine or reserving airline tickets felt more like using a computer program and less like slogging through a muddy network. The pages on those sites should pop up the instant I click, just like dialog boxes do on my PC.

You know what that means? That means it will be years—many years—before we have both the bandwidth and infrastructure to do any sort of "broadband" design on the Web. For the near future, we'll be optimizing our Web sites, squeezing every last byte from our pages, and doing whatever we can to make our sites load as quickly as possible.

Thank goodness, I say.

The Beauty of Being Slow

If you've done any amount of design or development on the Web, you're probably thinking I've lost my mind. Slow modems are a good thing? Lagging performance is a *benefit* to the Web?

Of course it is. Constraint propagates creativity. We're all forced to struggle with the issue of performance on our Web sites, but it is that struggle that breeds perspective on the Web as a medium. I've seen designers face this overwhelming roadblock over and over again—with the same result: *They do better work*. Without a doubt, constraint breeds creativity. I've been amazed at what can be done with two typefaces and colored table cells. You can do great work with virtually no bytes at all.

Where to start? Look to your competition for guidance. You know who your audiences is, and you know what other Web sites are vying for their attention as well. Do some analysis. See where the bar is. It's easy.

You can use a site like Web Site Garage (www.website-garage.com) to get a this information. It, and others like it, provide powerful tools for analyzing your site, including reports on how your site appears in search engines, how fresh the links are, and the total file size and download time of your pages. With a tool like this, you can track just how fast or slow your pages are. But it works just as well to point these sites at your competition. Find a few sites you

The 5-Kilobyte Interface

Creating fast Web pages is a lesson in constraint. Stuffing all the features, brand identity, and other requirements into an interface that loads quickly can be a frustrating experience at best.

Imagine, then, the nightmare of trying to fit an entire Web site into an unbelievable 5k. That was the goal of an innovative design contest held in the Spring of 1999, the brainchild of Stewart Butterfield. The rules were simple: "All HTML, script, image, style, and any other associated files must collectively total less than 5 kilobytes in size and be entirely self-contained." The entries, and in particular the winners, were remarkable. From e-commerce functionality to stunning visual design and even playable video games, the contest proved that constraint breads creativity, and that bandwidth can be a crutch.

Here are some of the winning entries.

The overall winner not only built an e-commerce interface in under 5k, but included a workable JavaScript shopping cart with a running total. Form and function blended with a great sense of humor.

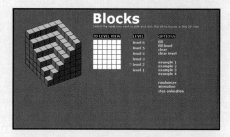

Caching images goes a long way when playing with blocks.

Remember the Atari 2600 home video game system? This entry evoked memories of early 1980s state-of-the-art games with fully functioning arcade action.

ASCII art to the max, this entry used Dynamic HTML animation to create a beautifully illustrated poem.

consider competitors, dump their URLs in one of these utilities, and see how they stack up. For example, if I were responsible for building a music site, I might collect the URLs of my competition, run them through the tests, and create a chart like this:

COMPETITOR	SIZE (bytes)	SPEED (seconds)
www.mp3.com	44,997	11.86
www.allmusic.com	80,380	23.14
music.yahoo.com	87,495	22.50
www.scour.com	165,361	46.41
www.wallofsound.com	97,261	26.62

This chart can serve as a target for my new interface. Clearly, if I want to compete on a performance basis with these sites, I'll need to build a home page that weighs in at somewhere around 95K—an average of the numbers above. With this exercise, I've set my goals for my home page. I should do similar studies for other key pages. How does my typical page of content match up? How about my search results page? Different functional pages will have different size specifications.

But this is only a guide. I now need to adopt a strategy based on performance. I need to find a way to scrape every byte out of my pages, and make them as fast as I possibly can.

Lighter sites are not just faster for the user, they're easier on the infrastructure, the support team, and the wallet.

Cutting the Fat with CSS

We've talked about the power of Cascading Stylesheets elsewhere in this book, but I'm going to bring that technology into this discussion as well.

The flexibility of Web technologies is certainly one of the reasons for their success. If you've done any amount of developing with these technologies, you'll soon realize that there seldom is one solution to any problem. Rather, there are typically any number of ways to accomplish something on a Web page, with any equal number of reasons to choose one over another. We can use this elasticity of Web technologies to our advantage when it comes to making our pages faster.

Let's look at a simple interface component from the music site I was talking about earlier. Here, you can see a list of musical genres, designed as a bulleted list with a subject header. The effect is a clean solution to the site's navigational needs.

Take a close look at the title bar of that box. Notice the thin border along the top? It's an elegant ornamental addition to the interface that helps define the box and give it a certain amount of visual weight. But look at the code it takes to design this title bar using just HTML:

The Economies of Speed

For large Web sites with lots of traffic, fast Web pages can mean more than just an effective user experience—it also translates directly into a significant expense. A 100k home page may not sound like all that much bandwidth to a company with huge digital lines, but when that page is accessed a million times a day (which isn't uncommon on the bigger portals and e-commerce destinations), it quickly adds up. Look at the math. One million multiplied by 100k means that just for the home page, you'd need to move 1,000 gigabytes of data. Cut 20 percent of the fat off the home page and you'll save the equivalent of a full T1 of bandwidth *per day*. An operations executive at one of the Web's larger sites once told me that each byte they included on their pages cost them 16 cents a year. Think about that the next time you add so much as a linebreak to your code.

And it's not just the fact that heavily used fat pipes are really expensive, but so are server farms, systems administrators, and network engineers. And you'll need more and more of them if you're running a heavy site with heavy traffic.

A simple navigation element from a music site. Easy code changes can dramatically reduce the amount of code it takes to generate something as simple as this box.

```
<TABLE width="100%" cellpadding=0 cellspacing=0 border=0>
  <tr bgcolor="#666666">
    <td>
      <img src="images/spacer.gif" width=1 height=1>
    </td>
  </tr>
</TABLE>
<TABLE width="100%" cellpadding=2 cellspacing=0 border=0>
  <tr bgcolor="#CCCCCC">
    <td>
      <font face="Arial,Sans-serif" size=2>
      <b>Browse By Genre</b>
      </font>
    </td>
  </tr>
</TABLE>
```

Looking through each line of markup, you can see how all of it is necessary. The first table draws the thin border. The table is set to extend the full width of its container, which in this case is the overall table that lays out the page. The `cellpadding`, `cellspacing` and `border` are all turned off to make the table as small as possible. A table row starts next, and sets the background to dark gray. Then, a table cell is filled with a single-pixel, transparent GIF image, because some browsers will collapse empty cells. I'd rather use a simple space, but the font size, even at the smallest size, will create too much vertical space.

Next, a second table creates the actual title area. This time, the table is given 2 pixels of padding so the text contained within the cell doesn't bump right up against its edges. The row then gets a lighter shade of gray, and the cell is filled with the appropriate title words, and wrapped in a font tag that takes care of the rudimentary typography. Finally, all the tags are closed and the title bar is finally done.

Now, compare all of this to a version designed using CSS:

```
<H3 class="title-bar">Browse by Genre</H3>
```

Alright, I'll admit to cheating on this one. The HTML is incomplete without the following CSS, located elsewhere:

```
.title-bar {
  font: bold .8em Arial, sans-serif;
  border-top: solid 1px #666666;
  background: #CCCCCC;
  padding: 2px; }
```

In this example, I've simply used a structural page element, in this case a heading, and given it a specific class of "title-bar," Then, in my stylesheet, I define exactly how I'd like it to appear. Let's take it apart.

The first line of this CSS declaration does my typography, like the font tag in the first example. Next, I ask the browser to simply draw a border along the top of the element, effectively throwing away the whole table plus the invisible image from before. Then, I set the background and add the padding. Done. And, it looks identical to the bloated HTML version.

But the benefits don't stop there. I can take the CSS for my title-bar class and put it in a separate document, then point from my HTML page to my external stylesheet like this:

```
<link rel="stylesheet" type="text/css" href="music.css">
```

Why would I want a whole separate document for my style? Well, primarily because I can now point to it from all of my other Web pages. And since the stylesheet never changes, the browser will just use the one from its cache. So once my users load one page on my site and get the CSS file, they can reuse it over and over again as they visit other pages, without incurring any additional downloads or using any more bandwidth. I get style for free!

Compared to the countless font tags and tables being downloaded over and over again in my old HTML version, this one is much faster and more efficient. But it doesn't end there. Every piece of code can be rewritten using elegant bits of style rather than blunt old presentation tags. Take, for example, the bullets in the navigation box we've been studying. See how they are a specific shape and shade of gray? Using HTML, this would be a luxury I'd probably do without, considering the code I'd need to do this:

```
<table cellpadding=0 cellspacing=0 border=0>
  <tr>
    <td>
      <img src="images/bullet.gif" height=12
      width=12 alt="bullet">
    </td>
    <td>
      <font face="Arial,Sans-serif" size=2>
      <a href="/rock/">Rock</a>
      </font>
    </td>
  </tr>
</table>
```

Again, a verbose table sets the stage for the effect I'm after. Instead of simply using the bulleted list available in standard HTML with the <UL> tag, I opt for more control. I want control over the specifics of the bullet, and HTML won't give it to me. So to get past that limitation, I use an image of the bullet I want. Nice and round and gray to match my interface. I need to put this image into a separate table cell since I want to control the wrapping of any list items that may get too long. By placing both bullet and text in separate cells, I can avoid wraps that look like this:

- A list item some times can
  get too long and wrap

See how the text on the second line wraps under the bullet? That looks sloppy and is hard to read. Rather, I use the two cells to achieve a cleaner look:

- A list item some times can
  get too long and wrap

So much work for such a simple effect. And consider that the code above is only for the first element in a list of over a dozen genres, and we start talking about a lot of stuff to download. Switching back to CSS, we throw almost all of the markup away and are left with stripped down and easy to read HTML:

```
<ul>
  <li><a href="/rock/">Rock</a>
</ul>
```

And the following entry in the stylesheet:

```
UL {
  font: .8em Arial, san-serif;
  list-style-image: url(images/bullet.gif); }
```

Now I can use the standard <UL> tag from HTML to generate the list, since I will get all the control I need. I still want to use my bullet image, but now I just specify it as the list-style-image in my CSS. This tells the browser to use a regular bulleted list (formatted with my typographic specifications, of course), but throw out the standard bullets and use my image in their place. I could use anything for a bullet now, and it wouldn't cost me any additional code.

As browsers get more powerful, designers will be able to do more with less. Early in the Web's history, designers eager for visual control of their pages used images to achieve these effects. In essence, they used bandwidth when under-powered browsers let them down. No font control? No problem! Just send your users an image of your headline. But we want to save bandwidth, not spend it on server connections to move pictures of words around. CSS lets designers send simple text with brief commands that accomplish the visual design goals while being incredibly fast.

And our pages can get even faster. There is a certain amount of magic involved here. Small pages can *feel* slow, while even the fattest pages can hold a user's attention, especially if you trick them into staying around.

The Illusion of Speed

There's a reason superstar magician David Copperfield fills his stage with scantily-clad women. It's not for the pure entertainment value, although I'm certain that's got a bit to do with it. And it's obviously not because they're attracted to the aging, bare-chested master of illusion. No, the answer is much simpler than that. These young sequin-clad women are there for one reason—so David can trick you into looking at them rather than noticing the rather mundane mechanics of performing sleight of hand.

It's one of the oldest tricks in the proverbial book: from street corner Three-Card Monte to the bump-and-pick techniques that relieve you of your wallet in the subway. Distraction leads to illusion. So why not use it to solve one of the most important problems facing Web designers today.

David knows that the majority of his audience will be distracted by the sparkly women while he busily makes an elephant disappear from the stage. While you may not be able to stomach the blatant sexism of Las Vegas shows, you can still exploit the effect on your pages—with a little work.

The goal is to get the most important part of the page on the screen as quickly as possibly, instantly giving your users something to look at while you go on to load the rest of the page.

HTML has historically been a very linear language. You started writing your page at the top, and continued to add words, images, and code until you reached the bottom of your page. Browsers reacted much the same way, displaying the content on the screen as quickly as the server sent it down the wire. We've been bound to what's been called the *flow model*. Pages can only be formatted along with the flow of the source code behind it.

In the very early days of HTML this meant that Web pages could have no columns or really any horizontal relationships between interface elements. Since the browser was simply reading code and displaying it on screen, pages were, by default, long lists of things—be them navigation links, paragraphs, or images. There was no way to arrange elements into a basic page layout. With the advent of tables in HTML, designers were at least able to add a basic sort of layout of these pages with an admittedly primitive system of rows and columns. If you were clever enough to figure out the intricate rows-pans, colspans, padding and spacing, you could achieve almost any layout.

Many of these table-based page designs are reminiscent of the Three-Panel Layout we discussed in Chapter Two, "Interface Consistency." But looking at that approach in the context of performance, there are some basic problems we need to solve. How many times have you visited a Web site only to be presented with a blank screen? You may notice that the browser's status bar is telling you that it is still working on getting the page. You sit and wait as the seconds tick by until suddenly, in an instant, the entire interface blinks onto the screen at once. Ever wonder why that happens?

Turns out that tables are a fairly difficult problem for browsers. There is a lot of math that needs to happen when you download a page. A table's cells are all sized based on their contents, as well as the contents of other cells around them. To do this work, a browser needs to know everything about the table before it can start to draw it on the screen. So it gets all the <TR> and <TD> tags, as well as all the stuff inside those tags, and then tries to figure out the most appropriate size for everything. When it finally finishes all of those calculations, it shows you the table.

The Three-Panel Layout, however, is typically structured as one large table. There will be a row across the top spanning the columns below, continuing brand identity and advertising. A second cell will run down the length of the page for navigation. Finally, a large cell on the right will house the page's content. The code would look something like this:

```
<table>
  <tr>
    <td colspan=2>
      <!-- Branding and Advertising in this cell -->
    </td>
  </tr>
  <tr>
    <td>
      <!-- Navigation in this cell -->
    </td>
    <td>
      <!-- This is the big content cell -->
    </td>
  </tr>
</table>
```

And the contents would show up in a browser window looking like a simple, standard Web page.

To create the specific layout effects, designers will often create pages that also include nested tables—meaning they contain additional tables within the overall structure. Nested tables slow the browser down even more, forcing the software to figure out each of the inner layouts before it can draw the overall page. Think about it—not only does the browser have to figure out what is in each cell in a table, now it has to figure out a whole separate table before it can get back to the one on which it was working. Of course, this doesn't mean you *shouldn't* nest tables within each other when trying to lay out your pages. But consider rethinking the design approach you're taking if you start approaching three levels deep—a table within the cell of a table, which itself is within a table. That's a lot of work for a browser to do, and your users will notice the delay in rendering speed, if not download time.

When a Three-Panel Layout is built with just one surrounding table, all of the code must be downloaded and processed before the page renders.

Thankfully, a simple addition to the <TABLE> element way back in Netscape 2.0 provides a simple solution to this problem. Much like images, you can align tables to the left or right. This allows separate tables to be positioned next to each other. So the Three-Panel Layout can throw away the surrounding table and create three separate tables for the top, left, and right. Then, by aligning the navigation table to the left, the content table will nestle up next to it and create a page layout identical to the first version. Identical, that is, except for the fact that each table gets drawn on the screen progressively. This new code would now look like this:

```
<table>
  <tr>
    <td>
      <!-- Branding and Advertising in this cell -->
    </td>
  </tr>
</table>
<table align=left>
  <tr>
    <td><!-- Navigation in this cell --></td>
  </tr>
</table>
<table align=right>
  <tr>
    <td><!-- This is the big content cell --></td>
  </tr>
</table>
```

With this simple reworking of the code, the user experience has been dramatically changed. The resulting code is now a bit larger, and would actually take longer to download. But rather than waiting for the whole page to pop up at once, users get to see something on their screens almost instantly.

They hit the page, and the branding and advertising table at the top is there waiting for them as the navigation starts to load. Then, as the navigation displays, the page content starts to load. It's sleight of hand. "Here, look at this while I do the rest of my trick…."

By paying special attention to the progressive rendering of content, we can create a sort of distraction for our users as they wait for their slow connections to suck content down to their computers. But the example above is still not ideal. Users of a site, after all, are primarily interested in the content

Now, the page appears exactly the same to users, but the experience of progressive loading is much more engaging.

of that site—whether that content is news stories, search results, items to buy, or whatever. They clicked a link expecting to be rewarded with either something that would satisfy their goal, or at least get them a bit closer. Yet the example above actually seems to be working in reverse. Content is the goal, but it is the last thing to show up on the page. Sure, my audience now has something to look at while the rest of the page loads, but wouldn't it be great if they could look at what they wanted during those first few moments?

We found ourselves in a similar situation when designing the Hotbot search engine's results page. A results page has a lot of jobs to do. Not only must it provide timely and accurate results to the user's query, but it must also offer a way of iterating the search, as well as provide relevant advertising to help offset the cost of providing a free service. Yet, the ultimate goal is to reward the user as quickly as possible. How, we asked, could we get the results on the screen as quickly as possible, while still maintaining the features and strong product identity our users expected from us?

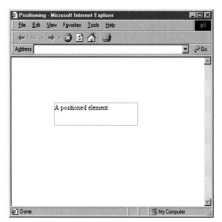

The answer was surprisingly simple. We solved the problem using a simple yet powerful feature of Cascading Stylesheets—namely the technology's ability to position elements on the page. Positioning was added as part of the second version of the CSS specification, and provides a way to do page layout much in the way desktop publishing programs like QuarkXPress and Adobe PageMaker do by allowing you to draw a box on a document exactly where you want an item to be, then pouring content into it. The code bellow illustrates just how simple it is to tell the browser exactly where you'd like a paragraph to be placed:

A paragraph can be placed and sized accurately using the positioning features of Cascading Stylesheets.

```
<p style="position: absolute;
  top: 100px; left: 100px; width: 100px; height: 100px;
  border: solid 1px red;">A positioned element</p>
```

Since we can position elements exactly where we want them, we can eliminate the aligned tables from the previous example and simply specify where each element should go. So, in our code, we simply positioned the brand and search interface at the top of the page, the advertising down the

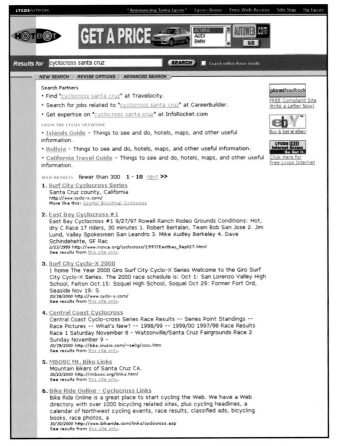

When we designed the results page for the Hotbot search engine, we used CSS positioning to alter the load order of the interface parts.

righthand column, and the search results in the center area. Here's the really interesting part: We put the positioned results as *the first thing in the page's source code*. Now the user experience is exactly what we were after. The page would shoot down to the user's browser and instantly display the search results in the right location on the page; then, the branding and interface would appear above them. And finally, after the meat of the page was displayed on the screen, the advertising would appear to the right.

You can do the same with your pages. Think of each element of the page as a discrete chunk of code. Take each chunk and wrap it with some CSS that positions it exactly on the page. Now, rearrange each chunk in the source so that it loads in the order that makes the most sense to your user. The browser is still displaying code in the order it loads, but the loading order has be changed because you can position the elements. The user experience is perfect—

Speed Metrics

Part of the problem with fixing slow Web sites is first figuring out how to measure just how fast they are. Total file size is a good start. If you can get your pages within a physical range of kilobytes, you'll be on the way to a faster interface. But kilobytes shouldn't be the *only* measure of performance. Especially considering the perception issues I've discussed in this chapter.

The ultimate goal of any performance strategy is to keep the users of a site engaged throughout their visit. For that reason, time may be a better metric than size. And by time, I don't just mean the math of modem speed divided by total kilobytes—that will be a theoretical number at best. Rather, a more appropriate indicator would be the total number of seconds between a click on a link to the user's perception of seeing information on the page. And the only way to get to that data is with a stop watch and a modem connection.

Even better, consider mapping out a few user tasks. Pick things appropriate to your site, like "completing the registration process" or "finding a song by your favorite artist to download." Then, measure in seconds the entire session, from typing in the URL to finishing the task. Do this with several users and find an average. Then try to make it faster.

the content loads first, and the shell begins to pop in around it. The elephant appears out of nowhere while the dancing girls dance.

There are drawbacks to this solution, of course. First off, this technique makes use of a technology only introduced in the version 4.0 browsers. That means that your pages will be a jumbled mess when viewed in older browsers. The only real solution to this problem is to use a browser detection strategy and build multiple versions—something I've discussed in detail in Chapter Five, "Browsers." Still, for all the complaining we've been doing about the browsers' CSS implementation, the positioning that I'm advocating here works nearly perfectly in all major 4.0 browser releases.

Another stumbling block may be the actual layout of your pages. Sometimes, to get the effect we need from a Web-based layout, we resort to such intricate HTML hacks that tearing apart our pages just to glue them back together with CSS just isn't a reality. For situations where it does work through, we can start to be creative in our design and give the illusion, at least, that the Web is a lot faster than it actually is.

Only after a rigorous study of how your users perceive your site can you be certain it is fast enough.

Designing for Slow

When bandwidth isn't an issue, when interfaces have no constraint, developers and designers lose track of the power of simplicity. Look back at the world of CD-ROM design a few years ago to see what I mean. Every user experience was different, every cursor was animated, it was a sea of full-screen color blends, drop shadows, and cyber-looking beveled edges—a mess.

Rather, embrace the constraint of slow connections. Fear big bandwidth. Learn to love the modem.

Advertising

When bandwidth isn't an issue, when interfaces have no constraint, developers and designers lose track of the power of simplicity.

[7]

With ad rates dropping at an alarming pace, and banner clickthrough falling

even faster, both advertisers and site designers are trying everything they possibly

can to get the hapless user away from his task at hand and into a commercial

message. From stretching stories across multiple pages to increase pageviews to ad

banners that mimic dialog boxes desperate for clicks, there is a harsh tension

between usability and revenue. Does it have to be this way? The Web differs

from other media in many ways, but its ability to collect detailed user informa-

tion and target that data is one way in which we can align the goals of both user

and advertiser. This chapter will look at these strategies for making advertising

actually compliment a user interface, and we'll explore the practice of building

User Profiles—a technique that can apply not only to advertising effectiveness,

but to building meaningful sites from a strong publishing strategy as well.

"You, sir, are an idiot."

Always a nice way to start the day; but I'm used to it now. Those e-mails generally continue with something like, "For someone who claims to know a little about the Web, you certainly don't use that knowledge on your dreadful sites. What were you thinking?"

I can understand the frustration. These flames always come from the same sort of person—logical, degreed, technologically savvy. They literally cannot understand why we've chosen to make our Web pages less usable just for the sake of a crummy ad banner. "What were you thinking?"

The Web is amazing. It's a wonderful expression of hypermedia, personal storytelling, and the interconnectedness of everyone on the planet. It's also an incredibly difficult place to make a living. With razor-sharp margins on e-commerce goods, plummeting ad banner performance, and an increasingly jaded and impatient audience, it's a wonder anyone can make ends meet with a Web business model.

Doing business on the Web—the ability to turn traffic into money—is affecting the very nature of how we design Web pages. And for better or worse, it's happening all around us.

Eyeballs = Money

The model has been a pretty simple one. For the few years that the Web has attempted to support a significant audience, people have been trying to fund it (and themselves) through a simple audience-publisher agreement that goes something like this: We'll give you our goods and services at no cost whatsoever, you look at banner ads and click on the interesting ones. The publishers pass production costs on to advertisers while users pay per click, absorbing brand messages in addition to the content they came to see.

Simple, right? Actually, it is. Advertising has always worked this way, whether in a newspaper, roadside billboard, or 30-second television spot. But there's a simple difference. On the Web, advertisers can tell if it's working and, more importantly, when it's not.

Historically, the metrics of advertising have been structured as "impressions" versus "performance." An easier way to think of this is how often a particular ad was viewed compared to how often the person viewing it acted in a measurable way. In the television industry, Nielsen ratings were compared to sales of a product or calls to a toll-free number. Print-based messages held up circulation numbers to other, simple measures of reader response. The Web, once again, changes everything.

Our Web servers do a great job of spitting out every painful detail of everything they do. This means we don't have to rely on the guesswork of other media to see how our products are doing. A magazine, for example, may offer two numbers to their advertisers: the literal number of subscriptions, plus a guess at the total reach, or how many times each copy is passed along to others to read. No need for that on the Web. We know exactly who surfed our site and when, with what browser at what address, and exactly what they looked at and for how long. We can also tell precisely which advertisements they saw, and which ones they clicked.

Imagine, for a moment, if television advertisers could tell when you changed the channel during commercial breaks, or when you hit the mute button, or got up to get a snack. Guess what would happen if they could get those statistics for every household with a television set. The model would collapse. Advertisers would obsess over the massive decrease in reach. They would petition television manufactures to stop including remote controls with their units. They would do absolutely anything to make you stay glued to the set.

Obviously, this is playing out today on the Web. The total number of online advertising impressions is skyrocketing. There is more Web traffic today than there ever has been; AOL and Yahoo page views per day only scratch the surface of the possible inventory a Web advertiser has to choose from. But the news isn't all good. Yield—a statistic derived from the number of impressions divided by the number of clicks to ad units—is falling dramatically.

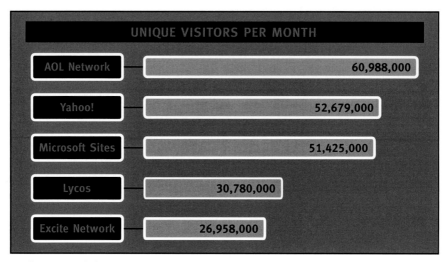

UNIQUE VISITORS PER MONTH

AOL Network	60,988,000
Yahoo!	52,679,000
Microsoft Sites	51,425,000
Lycos	30,780,000
Excite Network	26,958,000

Traffic is consolidating across the Web's largest sites, causing a decrease in advertising prices. As ad revenue drops, interface designs will need to be more creative when balancing audience and sponsors. These numbers are from MediaMetrix.com's September 2000 report.

Why is this? Two reasons: Traffic is a commodity, and the ads themselves are just so bad.

"We Interrupt This Message…"

So that's the state of the Web: Impressions are going up, yield is going down. The result? Advertising rates are dropping (because there's so much traffic to the big sites) while advertisers—still interested in the Web as a vehicle for brand promotion—are becoming increasingly unsatisfied with the keenly measured results of their campaigns. A very bad situation for those of us making a living turning traffic into dollars.

You can see Web sites responding everywhere you look. While traffic may be increasing, it's generally going to the massive portal sites like Yahoo, Excite, or Lycos, who, in turn, can undercut advertising rates. We're left with a vicious circle that cuts into the price sites can charge for their advertising. The rest of the Web, and the bulk of the commercial sites, must somehow increase traffic in order to stay alive.

Getting more people to come to your site is expensive, as is getting them to come more often. So how can you increase traffic? Change your interface. Give them plenty to click on and make them do it. Stretch out your content over multiple pages. The "Click Here for More" syndrome is running wild across Web interfaces, not because it's easier for users but because it generates more page views, thereby showing more ads. It's ease of use versus revenue. It's a tenuous balance.

But don't forget about yield—that magical number of banner impressions versus clicks. You can triple your page views, but if you don't skim enough of those users off the top and send them to your advertisers, you still won't be successful. Since the creative control of ad messages resides with the advertisers and not you, it means your interface once again must be sacrificed. Now, instead of constructing a visual hierarchy on the page that makes sense to the overall architecture of your site, you must interrupt the flow as often as you can with commercial messages.

I'm looking for computer-related commentary, but ZDNet wants me to check my horoscope. Is it any wonder advertising effectiveness is decreasing on the Web?

Here's a classic example. Surfing through an otherwise wonderful site, I was struck by the absurdity of untargeted advertising. I came to the page shown above, an interesting commentary on the future of the general-purpose personal computer. The advertisement, however, implored me to divert from my intended purpose and instead "Get my Horoscope!" Couple this with the fact that the ad sports a frustratingly deceptive interface—the text box and submit button are part of the image, and trick users into thinking they can act, when in fact they merely click through to the site.

My particular affinity for astrology notwithstanding, it was immediately apparent to me how easily it was for an ad banner like this to fail—distracting and annoying design, false interactivity based on deception, and completely inappropriate targeting. It's no wonder advertising on the Web is proving less and less effective with junk like this proving to be the norm rather than the exception.

"Click Here, You Idiot"

Most of us are often annoyed by advertising. Whether driving in our cars with the radio on or trying to get through the last two minutes of a football game, there comes a point when we've had enough. But commercial messages are as inevitable as death and taxes.

The same holds true for advertising on the Web, of course. If our industry's tenuous business models are any proof, reliance on advertising is something that won't be disappearing any time soon. So it's not surprising that some online advertisers are becoming dismayed with the ever-decreasing performance of their banners. We, as users, see so many ads that we simply ignore them. And that's not something advertisers can afford.

Therefore, some advertisers will go to any means necessary to get your attention. In fact, some will go as far as deception to gain your click.

Some advertisers I've spoken with say that consultants and agencies recommend banners that mimic operating system interfaces, because these ads increase clickthrough yield. So advertisers blindly submit ads that look like dialog boxes or download-progress indicators, aiming to trick people into clicking through to their sites.

Know what? In fact, they do work.

I've consistently seen clickthroughs on banners like this double or even triple the average yield across our sites. And the cycle perpetuates: Agencies continue to promote ads like this to their clients because the numbers prove they work.

Know what else? Clickthrough rates mean nothing.

In user testing, I've seen subjects fall for these deceptive banners again and again. They'll come to our search interface, type a query, and are presented with a "dialog box" that tells them their "Internet connection isn't optimized," or some such nonsense, and then an "enhancement" is supposedly downloaded. Users go for the Cancel button, but it sends them to the company's home page. They are confused and disoriented. They scan the page and suddenly realize what has happened. And then they immediately hit the Back button, often with a few choice words about the company. Is this the user experience the advertiser was after? Is this what click through is meant to represent?

Advertising should entice, not deceive. Good advertising is valuable to a targeted audience, and great advertising builds a relationship between customer and client.

Personally, I try not to start relationships with lies.

The Medium Is the (Commercial) Message

Television advertising works so well because it exploits the powerful aesthetics of the medium. TV ads tell us stories; they are 30-second narratives that evoke emotion and draw us in. Print ads, likewise, succeed by taking advantage of the information density allowed by that particular technology. So why are Web ads trying so hard to be what they aren't?

How many Web ads have you seen that try to emulate the emotion of television, or the depth of print? And how many of those are successful? Few attempts at providing an experience within the constraints of the banner have even come close.

Rather, Web ads need to exploit the very things that make the Web so interesting. We've already seen how the accountability of the Web has made advertisers nervous. But why aren't they leveraging that massive amount of behind-the-scene data? Ad targeting may be common today, but it's only in its infancy, and certainly it is not being exploited by the advertisers complaining the loudest.

The Ad Banner Hall of Shame

It is an unfortunate fact that short-sighted advertisers continue to pollute Web sites with banners designed to confuse and deceive users. Below are a collection of some of the worse offenders. These banners have been designed explicitly to mimic computer operating system interface elements like dialog boxes and search forms. The goal, of course, is to trick unsuspecting users into clicking. Some provide a false search interface that users will mistake for site functionality, other banners tell users something bad is about to happen, and offer a "cancel" button that navigates the poor visitor to the advertiser's Web site. Some use animation to trick users into thinking something is being downloaded to their computer, causing unsuspecting users to panic into clicking the offending material away.

Ironically, some of these screenshots were taken from a Macintosh. Not only do these banners attempt to deceive, but they also manage to offend users by not even bothering to offer them an experience appropriate to their operating system. Why so many advertisers attempt to fool new customers into their sites is a mystery. And considering the usability nightmare these nonsensical banners create, we can only hope this is a temporary fad.

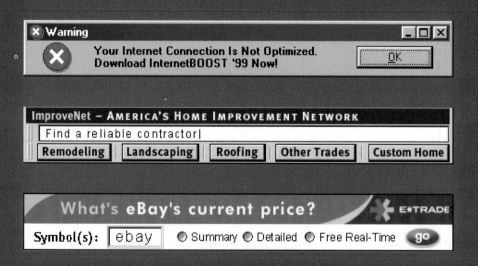

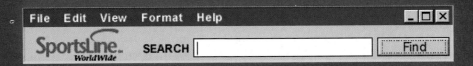

Of course, not every banner with an interface is deceptive. Some honestly try to provide a useful service within the narrow constraints of a Web-based advertisement. LinuxCentral, for example, ran a series of advertisements offering Linux aficionados the ability to sign up for a free newsletter without ever leaving the site they were visiting.

However, it's important to remember that even advertisements have usability standards. In the LinuxCentral case, for example, failing to actually type an address into the banner before submitting results in a less-than-elegant error message. The point remains: Advertising is often the beginning of a relationship with a new customer. First impressions are everything.

There's no excuse for untargeted advertising on the Web
today. There's no reason I should encounter a solicitation to
check my horoscope from a banner on a site offering commentary on the future of computing.

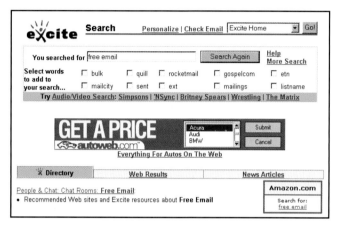

*Even though I explicitly tell the search engine I'm after free e-
mail, the site responds with an advertisement for a car. A
wasted ad impression.*

Do a simple search on any major search engine—try "free
e-mail"—and see how the advertising responds. When I
tried this on two competing sites, the results almost magically proved this point. I took a screenshot, above, of the first
site I tried. Searching for "free e-mail," I found that the
results weren't too bad, although you'll notice that none of
the results show up on my screen without scrolling. The
advertisement in this layout is the center of importance:
placed dead center on the screen with no distractions near
it, and surrounded by plenty of whitespace. But then the
inconsistency hits. Why would the most prominent part of
this interface, obviously designed to help me find resources
for free e-mail on the Web (since that's what I asked for),
lead me to searching for the price of a car?

The only possible corollary to an advertising strategy
like this in real-world advertising would be the highway
billboard. While I'm busy driving to the store, I notice sig-

nage on the shoulder telling me how wonderful the new
Toyotas are. Six months later, when buying a car, the ad
pops into my mind. Can you measure the effectiveness of
the billboard? Doubt it. But you can see why traditional
advertisers are befuddled by the lack of response by Web
users to their traditional approaches.

*Asking another search engine for free e-mail, I get the
response I'm after. It's no wonder well-targeted advertising
can increase yield by an order of magnitude.*

So I tried my "free e-mail" query on another search
engine. This time, along with similarly appropriate result
listings, I was presented with the simple, animated message,
pictured above. "Send and receive e-mail from anywhere on
Earth." Yes, Yahoo is advertising their own product. But
why not? The match is exactly what I'm after.

Getting Personal

So if targeted advertising works better, why don't more sites
use it. We've already discussed the difficulty small sites have
in generating revenue from their respectively little traffic. If
targeting ads proved twice, three times, or even an order of
magnitude more effective, then they could charge an appropriately scaled rate for these ads. Small traffic, plus a perfect

audience may actually keep the smaller sites (and the bigger ones, for that matter) alive and well. Is it really that hard to start matching a commercial message with a willing audience?

Of course not. Magazine publishers have long been able to target specific demographics and attract specialized advertisers eager to reach those eyeballs. Even television, especially with the explosion of cable and satellite channels, has been able to find higher-value niche audiences.

However, the Web excels at this. Even though surfing the Web is a fairly anonymous activity, there is a distinct trail of bread crumbs following each user of each site out there. Add to that the capability to meld that data with a wealth of past data plus any and every bit of information given explicitly by users, and even the smallest Web sites can provide appropriately functional commercial messages.

The trick is to know what data you can get, and how to do it.

Use your imagination again, and picture in your mind a big spreadsheet—like a new document in Excel. The rows of this spreadsheet have names in them. These are the users of your Web site. All of them are listed individually down the first column of your table. Now picture columns across the top, each labeled with a different thing that we either know or can figure out about each user. One might be labeled "browser version," another "zip code," maybe even "online stock trader?"

For each of your users you're building a profile. By building this profile, you can provide services that are created for each individual user, not the least of which is advertising that they actually find useful. Let's take a look at three different types of profiles in use on Web sites today:

- **Environmental.** Your site can and should make decisions about what to show your audience based on what the browsers and servers know about each other.
- **Preferential.** Users like to customized their surfing experience. What they tell you is critical… if you're listening.

- **Historical.** As users come back to your site, you should remember what they did the last time they were there, and make it easier to do that.

Environmental Issues

Every time you type a URL into your browser or click on a link, you're acting as a matchmaker. In essence, your telling your browser—the client—to politely introduce itself to a particular Web site—the server—and start an intimate conversation. Information is passed back and forth between the two until they strike up a friendship, form a relationship, shake hands, and a page appears on your screen. Think this analogy doesn't really apply? See it all the way to its logical conclusion: Uninstalling Internet Explorer from Windows is not at all unlike a messy divorce. But I digress...

Let's look at what is really happening as you surf the Web. And, more importantly, what that has to do with this advertising effectiveness we've been talking about.

Since the Web is, as we've seen, basically a collection of standards and protocols, it's not surprising that the way data is sent back and forth is done so in a consistent and efficient way. It's called the Hypertext Transfer Protocol and is shortened to HTTP, which you probably recognize from the Web addresses you see over and over again during your online travels.

HTTP is just a simple method for sharing information between servers and browsers on the Web. For this discussion, we're not particularly interested in how it really works. There are plenty of specifications and technical documentation that describes various jargon-filled network voodoo. For us, the really interesting part is *what* gets passed back and forth.

Getting back to our original introduction analogy, when your users first point their browsers at a server, a network connection is established. Almost instantly, the browser tells that server all about itself—it broadcasts what we'll call the *user environment*. First of all, it needs to tell the server where it is, via IP address, so it can send the requested page to the appropriate place. But there's more to it than that. The browser identifies itself, sending not only its particular brand name (Netscape Navigator, for example), but also which version (4.05), and which operating system it's running on (Win98). Suddenly, the server—or more importantly, you as developers and designers—know exactly what software your audience is using to visit your site, and where exactly they're coming from. Is this starting to sound familiar? This is the exact process we used in Chapter Four, "Behavior" to determine the screen resolution for sizing headlines. It's also how I suggested building appropriate interfaces for different users in Chapter Five, "Browsers."

You can start to fill in the little boxes in your spreadsheet for this user. You can look up her IP address, find out that she is surfing from a Fortune 500 company, and put a check in that box. You can tell she is using the latest version of her browser, and if she is coming to your from the ever-popular Windows operating system. No need to pitch Macintosh hardware in the ad banner, but considering their employer, a special offer on business travel may just get that click. The amount of information that passes between the browser and server can be amazingly deep. More little boxes to fill in with more interesting statistics about each and every member of your audience.

It gets really interesting, though, when they start coming back on a regular basis.

Building History

"Good morning!" says the woman behind the counter at the café as a wave of recognition sweeps across her face. "How was your trip to New York?" She reaches for my usual variety of caffeine and rings up the total all the while I'm blabbering on about this hip little Mexican restaurant in the West Village.

Now *that's* service, and it is the obvious sort of relationship that builds a strong business over time (and one of the reasons San Francisco residents so adamantly fight off national chains in their neighborhoods).

Understanding Cookies

It's funny how something that sounds so tame can cause so much controversy. But that's exactly the case with the often-misunderstood *HTTP Cookie*. The cookie is simply a little chunk of information stored on your computer by a server when you visit a site. For example, when you visit a site that requires that you enter a name and password for access (like a Web-based e-mail service), you'll often see an option to "Remember me in the future." Clicking that option allows you to skip the login process in the future. Behind the scenes, the Web server sets a cookie in your browser, which is then saved on your computer. In that cookie might be a unique identifier for you, so that when you return to the site, the server can ask for the cookie, look up your ID, and log you in. In the real world, it's very much like leaving your car with a valet. You give him your keys, he gives you a ticket. That ticket, like a cookie, allows you to get your car back when you return. It identifies you and gives you access to your valuables, while not associating you with any personal information.

The controversy surrounding cookies has two sources. The first is the misguided fear that cookies are an invasion of your privacy; that they allow unscrupulous Web servers to wander ad hoc through the private data on your computer. This is false, of course. Cookies can only be read by the sites that wrote them, and there is no other possible access to information stored on your machine.

The second, more imposing fear, comes from large advertising services like the DoubleClick Network. DoubleClick is a service that allows Web sites to include advertising banners without having to manage the scheduling, serving, and reporting. For the sites, it's a big win—they can simply outsource all of that work by including ads from DoubleClick's servers in their pages. The trouble comes from the fact that DoubleClick can then set a cookie when you visit a site. Say you visit a sports site, then a financial site, then a software download site. If all three sites are DoubleClick users (and increasingly, they are), then DoubleClick can tell what sites you've been to, and what you've looked at. DoubleClick, then, can build profiles of you across *all* the surfing you do. And this rightly freaks people out.

Just don't blame the cookies...

So why, after visiting the same dozen Web sites day after day, do none of them show a similar interest in my tastes and interests? Wouldn't it be a Really Smart Thing for them to shape and mold themselves progressively as I visit over and over again? Well, yes and no.

We'll take the "no" part first, which essentially boils down to the fact that it can be really hard to do.

Your Web site will have a lot of users: maybe thousands, maybe millions. They all visit you with one goal in mind. What is that goal? Who knows! They're all different and they all want some elusive thing from you. If you can keep your Web site simple enough that there's really no choice, then you're probably off the hook. If not, there's probably some work you could do here. Think of the difference between a site that simply offers a picture from a camera pointed at a fish tank versus a highway traffic site with dozens of cameras pointed at dozens of roads. You come to look at the fish and it's fun and strangely compelling—you can start to see a lack of geography in the Web and begin to understand the meaning of interconnected diversity. But that's it. You look, you're amused, you leave. The traffic site embodies many of those same feelings, but also accomplishes something the Web is exceptionally good at—providing crucially useful information at the exact time you need it. In other words, it provides appropriate functionality to a hungry audience.

But here's our simple theory at work. Every time you hit the traffic site, you have to follow the same clickthrough path to the particular views you want. Wouldn't it be wonderful if you could simply tell the stupid site which views you're interested in, have that site remember all of them, then let you return every day for an instant view of just how dreadful your commute will be?

Well, of course. And this particular strategy has been used ad nauseam across the Web, always designated with the prefix "My:" My Travel Agent, My Music Store, My Financial Portfolio, My Huge Boring Portal. It works. People love to customize a page, tweak the layout and color, and feel a sense of ownership. Naturally, it's a wonderful way to get people to invest in your site and build that retention so critical in building a traffic base necessary for success in the cutthroat business environment that we've been talking about. This is *preferential profiling*—building a relationship with your users based on what they've previously told you. MyNetscape, for example, asked me for my zip code when I customized the weather module in their interface. Netscape now knows where I live, and can target advertising to my region. Add to that, preferences like birth date for horoscopes, my financial portfolio, what sports teams I follow, and what TV channels I'd like listings for, and you've got a pretty detailed view of what advertising will appeal to me.

But there is something deeper you can do, often overlooked by those barreling ahead to build a customized version of their site. At first glance, it may seem like a creepy sort of Big Brother approach. I'll call this method *historical profiling*—tracking and remembering what a user has done in the past and using that to make discussions about what to do in the future. Good e-commerce sites, for example, will use a customer's past purchasing history to promote merchandise on future visits. A quick look at Amazon.com's home page shows this theory in practice. My Amazon home page will be very different from yours, even though I've not explicitly told them about my interests. I've simply

MyNetscape is a good example of preferential profiling. Users can customize virtually anything here, from the color to layout to specific details about the content. The result is a tailored Web experience for the user, and a detailed understanding of the audience for the site.

Amazon uses historical profiles to suggest other content (in this case merchandise) that also might interest me.

purchased enough books and music from them to allow them to infer my taste. Thus, a strange mix of Computer Interface books, Sea Kayaking Guides, and Monty Python movies greets me with each visit to the site.

Designing Good Advertising

Good advertising need not even look like traditional advertisements. There is no question that standard ad banners on standard Web pages can get lost. After all, users will only pay attention to so much periphery information on their way to accomplishing their desired task on a site. But what if that advertising was an embellishment of those goals? What if sponsors paid to promote themselves in the context of the functionality of a Web product?

In the print world, there is usually a clear separation of editorial content and advertising. Newspapers, magazines, and other printed materials will often go to great lengths to identify what was generated by the publication, and what has been paid for—but not always. Take as an example the business yellow pages in your local phone book. The functionality of those pages is perfectly clear: to connect you with business in your area. The architecture is one of alphabetical subjects, and the presentation is generally uniform. Uniform, that is, except for the merchants who have paid more for additional space. The phone book is designed and perceived as a comprehensive reference, but within that context is a business model that users of the book can respect and appreciate. Can the same hold true for Web sites?

Mapblast not only shows me where my friend's new apartment is, but lets me display where my favorite café is in relation. A paid sponsorship is unobtrusively filling the role of a site feature.

The Mapblast! Web site (www.mapblast.com) provides an interesting example. Offering an extensive suite of tools for generating maps, the site also integrates a sort of advertising as a tool. Drawing a map of, say, a friend's house in San Francisco, I can select a variety of neighborhood business to be added. Since we've decided to visit a café, I ask Mapblast to not only show where his house is, but where all the Peet's Coffee & Tea locations are. I could have selected from dozens of businesses to add to the map—from FedEx dropoff locations to RadioShack stores to my particular brand of ATM. Obviously, these companies are sponsors of the

Mapblast service. But it's interesting to see how brand messages and useful functionality can coexist in Web products.

When the goals of an advertising message match the goals of a user at a specific moment, the advertising will succeed. But Web sites need to move beyond simple keyword targeting, and begin to target based on user environment, history, and even preference. How much would our industry pay for a banner that drew a 50 percent click through? Enough to stop worrying about bulk traffic and sacrificial user experiences.

There are interesting implications for design. Good design comes from not only knowing your subject matter, but from an intimate knowledge of your audience. As it turns out, the same is true for good advertising. On the Web, then, targeted advertising and targeted user interfaces are the same thing. And the same profiling strategies can apply to both. But to fully exploit either, we'll need to think about Web design in a much more dynamic way.

Until then, we're stuck with ugly advertisements that don't work on sites desperate for traffic. Please, enough of the shotgun approach. Market to *me*!

Chapter Eight

Object-Oriented Publishing

The distinction between "design" and "programming"—or the even more disturbing nomenclature of "technical" and "creative"—is artificial. They are as intertwined as the art and science of Web design itself.

There was a time when all Web pages were simply text files on a Web server, formatted in HTML, and updated by hand. Building effective and manageable Web sites today requires dynamic, page-generating tools. From simple files to massive database-driven template systems, we'll look at how the basic process of design and development is changing. No longer are designers building mere pages. Rather they're working on creating effective interfaces that expose the power of content "systems." Design elements be combined and rearranged in infinite ways, making maintenance a breeze if designed with a deep understanding of the system from the beginning. And considering the cost of building and maintaining Web sites, this strategy might not be an advanced theory on the future of publishing online. It may be the only means for survival.

To be honest, Web design isn't all that glamorous. In fact, when I started in this business years ago my first job was, in essence, to be a human Perl script. I sat in a dark corner of the *Wired* magazine offices in San Francisco and if you asked someone what I did, they'd likely tell you, "Uh, I think he has something to do with our America Online area."

Each month, as *Wired* published its print version of the magazine, I would convert the work into something appropriate for our fledgling online outlets. I'd take a SyQuest cartridge (remember those?) full of QuarkXPress documents and strip the text out and save various copies into various directories. Then, I'd go through and convert each directory full of content into the correct format. We were experimenting with as many forms of electronic publishing as we could, trying to see just what would replace print when it died at the hands of the Digital Revolution. (Did I mention our zealous conviction that history had nothing to teach us?) One version added commands for AOL's publishing system that allowed us to upload files there. Another formatted the stories for our e-mail responder. And there was even a directory full of files in a strange new language called HTML.

I did these translations by hand at first. I would carefully open each file, add the appropriate formatting, and save out the file to the right location. As you can imagine, it was a process rife with error. The more files I would format at a time, the more mistakes I would make. I was, I suppose, only human. There were a couple of solutions, one of which entailed finding someone to do the even more mundane task of looking through the files scanning for mistakes. Rather, I started using macros on my Macintosh to format the files. I'd open a file with the plain text of a story, then select a macro script called something like "FormatFeatureForAOL," which would add the appropriate codes in the appropriate places, and then resave the file. Bingo! No more stupid formatting errors. My macros never got tired. They never forgot where they were in the process. They never made mistakes.

But why stop there? Wouldn't it be wonderful, I thought, if I could eliminate myself from the process entirely? Even though my files were now error free, I was still sitting in front of the computer for hours choosing the right macros to run and moving files to the correct servers. Then a guy a few desks over suggested something interesting. "Why don't you just dump all that text into a FileMaker Pro database? You could write a few scripts to run through and format everything and you'd be done."

So we did. I installed FileMaker Pro on my Mac and got some help setting up a simple database with some scripts for formatting the stories. The database itself had one "record" for each story, sort of like a recipe file—except that instead of a list of ingredients we had a collection of story parts: headline, author, date, content paragraphs. The scripts were pretty simple once we had pasted the stories into the right locations in the database; they were similar to the macros I'd used before. Each script would take all the pieces of a story and reassemble them into the differently formatted files I needed. The birth of a publishing system!

One day, a few weeks later, something clicked in my head. I had been running my little database for while and had a few hundred stories packed away in it. A few of us had been talking in a meeting about changing the way our rather primitive Web site worked (this was before HotWired.com even existed), and decided to add a few more links to each page on the site. The links would all point to the same pages, and would be identical for each story. It would mean not only changing the template for new stories, but also reformatting all the stories that were already online. "No problem," I said. "I'll just change the FileMaker script and re-run it on all the stories." Later that afternoon, we had those hundreds of stories updated and posted to the Web site. What would have taken days of copy-and-paste monotony was replaced with a couple hours of script tweaking and file copying.

Ah, hindsight. Looking back, I scratch my head and wonder why on earth we used such simple tools on underpowered machines. Wouldn't that be a job for Oracle running on a big Sun server? Maybe we should have given the magazine editors SGML authoring tools for document structuring and done post-processing to multiple output devices. At least we should have been using Perl.

Or maybe we had to take a few baby steps toward a dynamic publishing system with the tools we understood. Many of my friends in this industry have similar stories of days past. One built a template system using HyperCard; another used Lotus Notes. It didn't matter how comfortable we were with scripting or databases. It didn't matter which computing platform we were accessing. Everyone was trying to solve the same problem: How do you maintain a site that grows at the speed of the Web?

Getting Dynamic

Web sites face the same problems today. Sites continue to grow as fast as they ever did. The owners of these sites still change them as often as ever.

I call this process Object-Oriented Publishing. In the world of Computer Science, the term Object-Orient Programming (OOP) refers to a way of designing programs out of reusable objects in standard ways. For example, in a financial application, you might write an object that represents a check, with routines (called methods) that allow you to set the date, the recipient, the amount, and the memo information (which are known as properties). Each time you create a new check, it uses the same code to produce itself, to set/access its properties, and so forth. Object-Oriented Programming gets exciting when you start to think about just how much you can reuse the objects, not just in your programs but by exchanging objects with others. That way, when you sit down to write your financial application and discover you'll need a currency exchange, you can simply include one that someone else already has written and move on. (Well, in theory, of course. OOP standards may be well documented, but implementation of these standards is much like the reality I described in Chapter Five, "Browsers.")

Operating systems work that way too. If you're writing an application for the Macintosh OS or Windows, you don't need to write elaborate chunks of code to make a dialog box appear on screen. You can simply call the dialog box object and pass to it the things you want to appear on it.

I'm oversimplifying a very technical and abstract discipline, of course, but the principles are interestingly analogous to publishing systems on a Web site. Much like the simple FileMaker database and scripts that I used to publish the early *Wired* pages, sites today use databases full of content that gets pushed through templates to create Web pages.

Object-Oriented Publishing is lightweight. Dynamic Web sites are built using relatively simple scripting languages. Even if you have never attempted to write a line of code, you can see results almost instantly. We are not talking about compiling code or using debuggers.

I've spoken to a number of Web designers on all sorts of Web sites, and I've heard a common theme to many of their complaints. They talk about working with publishing systems or template languages in their organizations, but they feel completely cut off from how they work. "Oh, I can't change that part of my site," they say. "The programmers take care of that."

If there is one important thing you should take away from this chapter, it is that anyone—anyone—can participate in the development of dynamic Web sites. The distinction between "design" and "programming"—or the even more disturbing nomenclature of "technical" and "creative"—is artificial. They are as intertwined as the art and science of Web design itself.

For this reason, we're going deconstruct an Object-Oriented Publishing system behind a relatively simple site. I could have chosen a large-scale commercial content site, or an e-commerce powerhouse with a triple-digit stock price.

Instead, we're going to look at a small site from a Presbyterian church in San Francisco, California. This site faces the same problems as many others: With limited staff and resources, how can this organization maintain a Web presence that can expand quickly yet still present a professional and organized look?

A simple Web site for a church in San Francisco. Yet it uses the same publishing techniques as some of the largest sites on the Web.

The site is not terribly complex, yet there are a number of pages that need to be maintained by a staff unfamiliar with the peculiarities of building Web sites. To accommodate the desire for an organized look and feel, the site was developed using a series of scripts that run on the site's Web server. This ensures consistency across the many pages of the site, while freeing the church's staff to focus on developing the content.

One of the goals of this Web site was to act as a repository for the sermons delivered during weekly worship services. Adding a page or two a week to a simple Web site may not seem like a very time consuming task, but there are quite a number of fairly technical steps involved—converting the Microsoft Word file of the sermon to HTML, ensuring proper navigation and branding exist on each page, transferring the file to the right place on the Web server, etc. In fact, the church was facing the very publishing problems we faced at *Wired* magazine years ago—the same problems shared by most any Web site wishing to update with any regularity.

Looking at how the church solved this problem is an excellent primer to Object-Oriented Publishing. We'll start with an introduction to the entire process, then drill down into each part, using the church's sermon archive as an example. In the end, it should be clear just how easy it can be to get started with a system like this, and what the implications are for good Web design.

To start, we need an understanding of the process. Below, I've outlined the basic steps for creating a Object-Oriented Publishing system.

1. Strip your content of all formatting.
2. Figure out what the pieces are.
3. Store those pieces in a database (or something similar).
4. Design some templates.
5. Wire it all together.

We're going to follow these steps as we develop a basic publishing system for Calvary Presbyterian Church's Web site. In the end, we should have a virtually maintenance-free site that can be updated by someone with even the most basic computer skills.

Naked Words

Before we can even think about what the pages are going to look like, we need to understand exactly what the content is. In the case of the sermons, the structure of each piece of content (or the *schema* to use database jargon) is pretty well defined. Each sermon was sent to the site's manager as a Microsoft Word file with the following information:

- **Title**: What the sermon was called. Essentially a headline.
- **Pastor**: Who wrote and delivered the sermon.
- **SermonDate**: When the sermon was delivered.
- **Text1**: A passage from the Bible that accompanied the sermon. Not the actual text, but a pointer consisting of book, chapter, and verse.
- **Text2**: Often, there would be a second passage.
- **Body**: The paragraphs of content.

The process of identifying and labeling each component of a story is critical to the eventual success of a system like this. In time, we'll be using these little pieces of each sermon to design templates and create navigation. Think about the pages on your Web site and how the content could be broken up into little pieces. For example, if you are responsible for job postings on a corporate site, you might develop a schema like this:

- Job Title
- Department
- Description
- Open Date
- Requirements
- Salary Range
- Contact

Or, if you're developing an e-commerce site, each product page might have a schema like this:

- Item Name
- Description
- List Price
- Price
- SKU Number
- Shipping Options
- Current Stock

You get the idea. This is simply a process of defining the content you'll be using at as fine a grain as practical. I suggest being as explicit as possible. Write down all the pieces just like I did above. Think about all the possibilities for the content. In the first example, could a sermon ever have more than two Biblical passages associated with it? If so, I'd need to make a note of that now. Describe each one as clearly as possible, including what type of data it is: Date? Number? Text?

Thinking About Architecture

It's time to do some technical work now. We're going to take the schema we just documented and create a database to hold the content. But before we do that, it pays to take a quick overview of how systems like this really work.

You may have heard the term "three-tiered architecture" thrown around in the past. This is simply more jargon for an overall structure of system design. When applied to the type of system we're developing here, a three-tiered architecture means something fairly specific: It refers to the basic components of an Object-Oriented Publishing system. Here are the three tiers:

- **Backend Database**: This is where the content is stored. Some popular databases include Microsoft SQL Server, Oracle, Sybase, and the open source MySQL.
- **Middleware**: A server-based application that processes requests for pages and provides a scripting language for writing templates. Some popular middleware packages include Microsoft Active Server Pages (ASP), Allaire's Cold Fusion, and the open source PHP. We'll talk more about these a bit later.
- **Interface**: This refers to the HTML code that gets sent to your users' browsers.

I'm writing this on a relatively standard laptop running the Windows 98 operating system. Also running on this machine is Microsoft's Personal Web Server (which includes the ability to process ASP templates) and the Access database software that ships with Microsoft Office. All of this software is readily available and either free or relatively inexpensive, which is why I chose it for this demonstration. I wanted to provide an example that you could recreate on a standard PC. Obviously, you would never use Microsoft's Personal Web Server for a site with any amount of traffic—and there are dozens of other choices for each option above. Ultimately, the process for choosing the right pieces is complicated and specific to every Web site. It's the reason why we pay our Chief Technology Officers so much.

Just remember: *Anyone* can experiment with dynamic publishing. This isn't just the domain of engineers, database analysts, or any other IT professional. Getting started is simple. The principles and techniques are easy to understand. You can install the tools on your personal computer and appreciate how it works from the inside. It will make you a better designer.

Database Design

Let's get started building the system. Since I have the schema for the sermons defined and documented, I can now create a database that will mimic it. That way, I'll be able to store all of this content in a well-structured place and know exactly what to ask for when I want to get it out again. Since I put the effort into the schema, this will be a relatively painless process. I start Access and create a new database, then add a new table (see the sidebar, "Database Vocabulary").

Now, I simply add fields to the table in my database. Like I said, this is pretty easy, since I documented my schema first. I add each one and give it the appropriate properties. One important note: I've added an additional field labeled "sermonid," given it a type of "AutoNumber," and made it the table's Primary Key. This all means that

Database Vocabulary

Even if you never create your own database, you'll likely find yourself collaborating with someone who will. It's important to know how they are built, and what the pieces are called. Here's a crash course:

Database: Think of this as the container that holds everything. It is not the program you use, even though people often misuse the term (just as a word-processing program is not the report you write). Specifically, a database is the file a database program saves out.

Table: Databases store their content in tables, and there can be many of them. A table looks similar to a spreadsheet, rows of information categorized into columns. Tables can be joined each sermon in the sermons table will get a unique number assigned to it when the content gets added. That way, when

I start to put templates and pages together later, I'll be able to ask for specific sermons by an ID number that gets automatically assigned by the database.

Next, I can start adding some content. It's very important to strip any and all formatting from the text at this point.

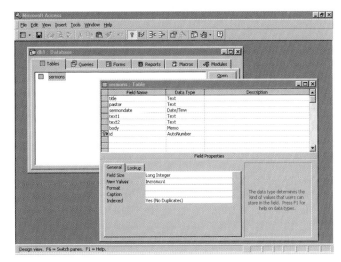

Adding fields to an Access database.

All I want in my database is plain text—not Microsoft Word formatting, no HTML tags, nothing. All the presentation information will be applied through a template a bit later. For now, I want the content to live in my database in as pure a form as possible.

together for lots of power. More on that later in this chapter.

Fields: Each individual intersection of a row and column in a table is called a field. A field can be given properties like how much data it can contain, what type of data is allowed, or if the field must be filled in or not.

Schema: The names and types of all the tables and fields. More generally, "schema" refers to the overall structure and design of a database.

Query: To get at the information in tables, you need to ask for it. In the lingo of databases, this is known as a query. Databases expect very specific instructions on what they should be spitting out.

SQL: Stands for Structured Query Language, which is made up of commands that you can use to ask the database for information, or send other commands to delete data, copy data, or do a variety of other tasks.

To get the content into the database, I just copy and paste the appropriate parts of a particular sermon's Word file into the appropriate fields.

Fragmented Thoughts

As I mentioned earlier, I'm running Windows 98. On the CD-ROM that came with my system, I found the installation option for Microsoft's Personal Web Server. I installed it on my machine and can now serve Web pages to the rest of the world. More importantly, I can write pages embedded with scripts intended to be run on a Web server (as opposed to the scripts I wrote in

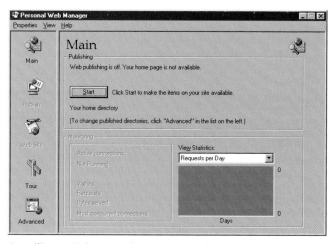

Installing a Web server is as easy as clicking "Start." Now I'm ready to build a few dynamic pages.

Chapter Four, "Behavior," which run in the browser).

Once the server is installed, using it is a matter of point and click. And once I've clicked the "Start" button in the control panel, I can start building the site.

I'm going to start with a few existing pages for the moment, and leave the database work for later. In the first screenshot of the church's Web site, you may have noticed a navigation area near the top of the page. This navigation bar points to thing like "Activities," "History," and "Staff." Those pages already exist as plain-old HTML. However, I'm going to do a little bit of work to them to ensure they stay maintainable. Looking at all those pages, I see that they follow a similar layout: They all share the same header with navigation and search. Before this project, I would have had to edit each and every HTML file to make the simplest change to the top of the page while still hoping to maintain consistency across all the pages. For example, when the church added a search engine, someone had to copy and paste the search interface code into the dozen or so pages that make up this site. Not a big deal for a site this size, but how big is yours? Some of the commercial sites I've worked on have had upwards of 100,000 pages. That's a lot of copying and pasting.

The alternative is to create *one* header and include it in each page. With static HTML pages, this isn't possible. But I'm no longer working with static pages. Rather, I'm going to use one of the simplest functions of any middleware package: the virtual include. First, I cut out the top of every page on the site—everything from the beginning of the file through the <BODY> tag—and paste it into a separate file. I've called this new file "header.inc" and put it in an "includes" directory. Then, where I cut out the code from the original files, I add this bit of code:

```
<!--#include virtual="/includes/header.inc"-->
```

Now, before the server sends the file to a user's browser, it will notice that line and grab the header from the includes directory and merge it with the HTML page. The

Server-Side Includes

Interested in harnessing the power of consistency using "includes," but without all the complexity of a full dynamic publishing system? You're not alone. Once Web designers see just how simple SSI can be, they jump at the chance to automate their interfaces.

Most Web servers have the ability to do virtual includes right out of the box. The open-source Apache Web server, for example, has the capability to do some interesting and fairly advanced includes and even basic conditional logic simply by turning on "server-parsed pages" in its configuration files. Ask the administrator of your Web server (or consult your server's documentation if you're going solo). You may be able to start reaping the design benefits of simple server code right away.

result to the user will be seamless. Now, if I decide to make even the slightest change to the header, I simply edit the included fragment. The change is automatically reflected in *every single page on the site*.

Creating Templates

Simple pages, simple code. Let's add a bit more complexity to this project. At this point, I've copied and pasted about a dozen sermons from Word files into the Access database. Now, I can create a template that grabs the content out of the database, wraps it in my interface and design, and sends it off to my users' browsers.

I start the template just as I did with the previous pages by including my standard header. These pages need to look like every other page on the site. But that's where the similarity stops. These pages are different because they really don't exist. What I mean is that I'm actually going to be creating what appears to my users to be dozens of new pages, but it will actually be just one template pulling content from the database I created earlier. I'll explain this more by example.

First off, we need to open a connection to the database and ask for some content. Each middleware package has its own unique way of doing this. In fact, Microsoft's ASP technology has several ways to accomplish this. Again, it's important to remember here that the syntax for what we're

Code by Any Other Name...

The ASP code in the examples in this chapter are mixed right in with the HTML that will eventually get sent to the browser. For this to work correctly, the server needs to look through the page before it sends it, and act on any scripts that need to be executed. In the case of ASP, these scripts are set off from the HTML by using the angle brackets (much like HTML) but with percent symbols between them. Thus:

```
<% ASP code in here gets executed on
the server %>
```

The open-source middleware package PHP uses a similar technique, but replaces the percent symbols with question marks:

doing is almost irrelevant. What matters most is the overall architecture of this system. I'm going to create something called a Server Object that will let me connect to the Access database of sermons, then enable me to build a page with the results.

```
<OBJECT RUNAT=Server ID=Conn
PROGID="ADODB.Connection"></OBJECT>

<%
Conn.Open "Calvary"
Set RS = Conn.Execute(SELECT * FROM sermons WHERE
sermonid = 1)
%>
```

The first line simply tells the server to open a connection to the database. The `<OBJECT>` tag is similar to the one you may have used to include video or Flash in your Web pages. The exception here is the `RUNAT=Server` attribute, as you would expect, creates the object on the Web server rather than in the browser. The next couple of lines start the communication process with the database. `Conn.Open` tells Access that we're after the `Calvary` database, where the sermons are stored. The next line fills a variable with the results of our first query. In this case, we're sending some SQL commands to the database, asking for the following,

```
<? PHP code in here gets executed on
the server ?>
```

Cold Fusion uses tags surrounded by angle brackets, mimicking the syntax of HTML, but starts every server-side tag with the letters CF:

```
<CFTags>Get executed on the server
and can take parameters</CFTag>
```

It's worth repeating, though, that when you get past the different formats for the various scripting languages, they all do the same things. Each one of these server-side languages have their own particular strengths and weaknesses, but ultimately once you learn one, you'll understand how they all work. Keep that in mind the next time someone argues about the "world's best language."

"In the Calvary database, please find (SELECT) all the fields
(*) from the first row (sermonid=1) in the specified table
(sermons)."

Now I've got the RS variable full of the content I origi-
nally pasted from my Word file into the database. The rest
of the template consists of my HTML with variables where
the content should be. So let's get some of this content
onto the page.

```
<h1 class="title"><%= RS("title") %></h1>
```

Since the top of the page is already taken care of by
using our included header fragment, I can move directly
into the guts of the page. Here, I've added a headline
(<h1>), and then printed the title that came from the database. Now, when the server processes this page, it will sub-
stitute the variable with whatever is in the database field
title in the row starting with sermonid=1. Notice how this
variable maps exactly to the fields I added when I created
the Access database, which in turn maps to the schema I
developed at the very beginning. In fact, using ASP, my
whole schema is available to me:

```
<%= RS("title") %>
<%= RS("pastor") %>
<%= RS("sermondate") %>
<%= RS("text1") %>
<%= RS("text2") %>
<%= RS("body") %>
```

So the rest of the page is easy:

```
<div class="pastor"><%= RS("pastor") %></div>
<div class="sermondate"><%= RS("sermondate") %></div>
<div class="text1"><%= RS("text1") %></div>
<div class="text2"><%= RS("text2") %></div>
<div class="body"><%= RS("body") %></div>
```

This code is optimized for a browser that supports Cascading Stylesheets. Each of these variables could have been surrounded by a <TABLE> and numerous <FONT> tags. And, since I'm using a dynamic publishing system, I could very well create separate versions of this code for separate browser versions and simply serve the appropriate one. But I wanted to show here the connection between my original architecture, the database structure, my template code, and the interface code. Notice how well all of the different pieces tie together. Just as the variable names match the database fields, the class names that reference CSS declarations match as well. Since I was very specific in how my content was structured at the instigation of the process, the whole system can grow from a solid foundation. Good design doesn't start with page layout. Good design starts at the beginning.

I'm not quite finished with the template, however. Since I have a complete scripting language at my command, I can manipulate a few things to get them exactly the way I want them. For example, the date coming out of the database isn't terribly attractive as "11/16/2000." A bit of code fixes that:

```
newdate = FormatDateTime(RS("sermondate"), vbLongDate)
```

This takes the date from the database and passes it to a built-in function called FormatDateTime, which does exactly what you'd think it does. In this case, I've asked it to set the date in one of the predefined formats: vbLongDate gives me "November 16, 2000".

I need to do a similar transformation on the body content, since it lives in the database without any tags at all. Since each paragraph in the body has line breaks between them, I can replace them (using another eponymous built-in function) with <P> tags to show the paragraphs in the browser:

```
replace(RS("body"), vbcr, "<p>")
```

And on and on. I can change anything I like, or use logic (if...then...else statements) to make my template even smarter. For example, if a particular sermon only has one Biblical passage associated with it, then we only need to show one in our template. We can check and see if anything is in the `text2` variable, and only show the surrounding HTML if something is in there:

```
<%if RS("text2") = "" then %>
  <!-- No code here -->
<% else %>
  <div class="text2"><%= RS("text2")%></div>
<% end if %>
```

Reusing Chunks

The example so far only does one thing: It pulls one pre-specified story from the database and runs it through a formatting template. What about all the other sermons? How will I get them out of the database?

First, I need to add a way to reuse my template over and over again for each sermon in the database. Remember that SQL command I used to ask the database for the content?

```
"SELECT * FROM sermons WHERE sermonid= 1"
```

I need to replace that `sermonid=1` with a way to say, in essence, "sermonid can equal anything." For this, I'll use the URL, or, more specifically, the query string part of the URL.

```
http://www.calvarypresbyterian.org/sermonDisplay.asp?show
sermon=1
```

You may have seen URLs like this before. They point to a server and a specific page, but then they follow that with a question mark and one or more variables with values. Everything following the question mark is called the query string. Here, I've created a URL that sets a variable named `showsermon` to the value of "1". Now in my template, I can

ask the server to put whatever it finds in the query string
into a variable I can use on my page:

```
showsermon = Request.QueryString("showsermon")
```

Now my template has a variable named `showsermon` with
a value of "1". Next, I use it in my SQL statement:

```
"SELECT * FROM sermons WHERE sermonid=" & showsermon
```

From there, I can change the number in the URL and
automatically show the corresponding sermon from the
database. So if I send users to…

```
http://www.calvarypresbyterian.org/sermonDisplay.asp?show
sermon=2
```

they'll see a nicely formatted page with the second sermon
in the database. And…

```
http://www.calvarypresbyterian.org/sermonDisplay.asp?show
sermon=3
```

will show them the third. One important note: In this
example, there are only three sermons in the database. If a
user were to change the number in the URL above to a "4"
or higher, bad things would happen—most notably they
would get an ugly error. Well-written, robust code should
always include routines that handle errors like this, but I'm
leaving them out for the sake of clarity in this system.

Let's see what I've got so far now:

```
<OBJECT RUNAT=Server ID=Conn
PROGID="ADODB.Connection"></OBJECT>

<%
  showsermon = Request.QueryString("showsermon")

  Conn.Open "Calvary"
  Set RS = "Conn.Execute(SELECT * FROM sermons WHERE
  sermonid=" & showsermon)
%>

<!--#include virtual="/includes/header.inc" -->

<h1 class="title"><%= RS("title") %></h1>

<div class="pastor"><%= RS("pastor") %></div>
<div class="sermondate">
  <%= FormatDateTime(RS("sermondate"), vbLongDate) %>
</div>
<div class="text1"><%= RS("text1")%></div>
<%if RS("text2") = "" then %>
  <!-- No code here... -->
<% else %>
  <div class="text2">
    <%= RS("text2")%>
  </div>
<% end if %>

<div class="body">
  <%= replace(RS("body"), vbcr, "<p>") %>
</div>

<%
  RS.Close
  Conn.Close
%>

<!--#include virtual="/includes/footer.inc" -->
```

Reviewing my template, I find the following to be happening: I'm instantiating an object on the server that lets me talk to a database named `Calvary`. Once I open the connection, I ask for all the fields in the table `sermons` from the row that has a `sermonid=1`. Then I start putting things on the page. I start with my page header, which I include from a fragment file. Then comes the headline, pastor's name, and sermon date (which I've reformatted to my liking). After that, I put down the first passage, and then check to see if there is a second. If not, I show nothing, or else I print the code. Then, I add `<P>` tags to the body and show that as well. I send two commands to the database object, telling it to close the connection. Finally, I include a second fragment—the page footer with a copyright notice and other information—at the end of the template.

That's it. That's how easy it is to start building a basic database publishing system.

Building an Index

If I were creating this project out of static HTML, I'd now have to take all the sermon pages and copy and paste relevant information from them into an index page. I'd probably want to show the date, the title, and the author of each one. I'd also need to include the URL in an `<A HREF>` tag to provide a pointer. The end result would look something like the screenshot on the next page.

But this isn't a static HTML project. All that information is sitting in the database waiting to be used; or, in this case, reused.

I start with a very similar template as before. I open the database connection and send some SQL asking for the appropriate content. Then I include the page header and display the results. Only this time, the SQL is different:

```
Set RS = Conn.Execute("SELECT sermonID, title, pastor,
sermonDate FROM sermons ORDER BY sermonDate DESC")
```

A list of all the pages available, organized as a navigable index.

You can see that I'm no longer asking the database for every field. In my last SQL statement, I told it to SELECT *, which means, "All Fields." Now, however, I'm asking for specific fields: sermonid, title, pastor, and sermonDate—still from the table sermons. I could ask for them all, but since I have no intention of using the body field, and because it's such a large field, my page will perform faster by being more specific. There is one other difference between this SQL statement and the previous—that is, the ORDER BY command.

This takes the results of my query, which will come out of the database in no particular order, and rank all the rows by date. The DESC means descending. I could have otherwise specified ASC to reverse the order.

The RS variable now has a lot of stuff in it. It's holding all the IDs, titles, pastor names, and dates of each sermon in the database. My template needs to arrange this data into a nice interface for my users. To do this, I'll put everything in a table, starting with some headers for each column:

```
<TABLE BORDER=0>
  <tr>
    <th>Date</th>
    <th>Sermon</th>
    <th>Pastor</th>
  </tr>
```

Then I'll start a loop that runs through all the results I get back from my query, printing each variable as it comes to it:

```
<% Do While Not RS.EOF %>
  <tr>
    <td class="sermondate"><%= RS("sermondate") %>
    </td>
    <td class="title">
<a href="sermonDisplay.asp?id=<%= RS("sermonID") %>">
    <%= RS("title") %></a>
    </td>
    <td class="pastor"><%= RS("pastor") %></td>
  </tr>
<%
  RS.MoveNext
  Loop
%>
```

There are some interesting things going on here. First, I add a line of code that tells the template to loop through all the results until it runs out of results, or `While not RS.EOF` (which stands for the "end of file"). At the end of the block of code, I tell it to move to the next set of results (`RS.MoveNext`) and the `Loop`. This will create row after row of a table, but since I put this loop below the first `<TR>`, only one header.

I'm still using the same class names for my CSS as before, carefully matching them to the variable names to keep everything clear. Each cell in the table now contains the replaced value of each variable. The result is a well formatted table of contents to all the sermons in the database.

One final note of interest here. In the second cell of the table, I'm displaying the title of the sermon. I'm also using that page element as the navigational link to the actual sermon. To do this, I've included part of the URL in the `<A HREF>` tag, and used the `sermonid` variable from the database to generate the rest of the address. As the template loops through all the results of the query, the URLs automatically are assembled to point to the correct sermon in the database:

```
<a href="sermonDisplay.asp?id=<%=RS("sermonID") %>">
```

The system is essentially complete. All the sermon pages are identically formatted, creating a clean and consistent interface to an ever-growing archive of content. That archive is accessible through a nearly automatic index pulled from the same reusable fields of the database I used for displaying the sermons. Maintenance is a breeze. Want to change the design? A quick template edit updates the hundreds of existing pages on the site. Find an error? Change it in the database and it updates wherever it appears—on a sermon page, in the index, on the search results page.

Eternally Current

I'll add one final feature to this little system that demonstrates another aspect of the power of Object-Oriented Publishing: keeping archives fresh.

On the sermon template, I'm going to create a box on the right margin of the page that shows the last five sermons that have been added to the database. That way, no matter what sermon you happen to be looking at, the page will always feel like part of a Web site that is kept up to date. The implications for a sense of history, however, create an interesting design paradox.

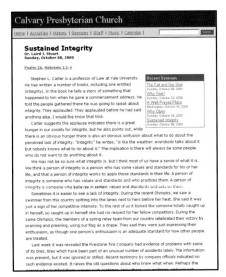

To start, I'll take my existing template, and add a simple one column table aligned to the right of the body copy. In that table, I'll list the additions to the site. When we're finished, it should look something like the screenshot to the right.

The table structure itself is easy to create, especially since I'm doing all the presentation (fonts, borders, backgrounds, etc.) using a stylesheet. Since we'll be pulling the content of the table out of the database, I'll leave that area blank for now.

Now every sermon in the database— no matter how old—can point to the latest content.

```
<table width=200 cellspacing=0 cellpadding=0 align=right>

  <tr>

    <td valign=top>

      <!--Table content goes here-->

    </td>

  </tr>

</table>
```

I'd also like the flexibility to use this little interface component elsewhere on the site. It might make a nice feature for the site's home page, for example. To build in that capability, I'll put this code in a separate file to be included in the template, and then add the include directive in the right place:

```
<!--#include virtual="/includes/recent_sermons.inc" -->
```

Of course, now I can simply add that line of code anywhere on the site to add the feature. The more features I create, the more flexibility I get for my site, while still making maintenance and consistency realistic goals.

Now, to get the content out of the box, I'll repurpose the SQL commands I used on the index page, but with a slight difference. I'll still be opening a connection to the database and requesting content from the sermons table, but this time I need even less data than before. I'm also changing the name of the variable that stores all that information to latest from RS so that they don't collide with one another.

```
<%

  Set latest = Conn.Execute("SELECT sermonID, title,
  sermonDate FROM sermons ORDER BY sermonDate DESC")
%>
```

So once again, I've got a variable full of data to display on the page. This time, rather than creating a perpetual loop that waits for the end of the file, I'll set up a loop that counts to five, showing each line of my mini-index, and then stops.

```
<% for y = 1 to 5 %>

<div class="recent_title">
<a href="sermondisplay.asp?id=<%=latest("sermonID")%>">
  <%= latest("title") %></a>
</div>
<div class="recent_date">
  <%= latest("sermondate") %>
</div>

<%

  latest.MoveNext
  next
%>
```

I've created a simple object that I can include in any page, but what's more interesting is the effect it has on each page. The sermon archive on this site spans five years worth of content. But now, the content of each page—regardless of age—is embellished with an up-to-the-minute accurate feature. It is as if I was updating every single page in the archive every time someone adds a new sermon to the database. Of course, you *could* do something like this by hand, but the labor would be prohibitive. You would literally spend all your time maintaining your site, at the expense of creating new content and features.

Systems like this also have an interesting historical effect on the pages they contain. If I decided to, say, change the background color of every page, or use advanced scripting for a feature, or whatever, I would be changing *every* page. The implication, then, is that the pages will cease to reflect the visual design and technological advances of the era in which they were created. For example, when I was studying history in college, I would scour editions of *Time* magazine dating from the late 1800s while doing research. Much of the value of these sources was not only in the content of the articles, but the context in which they were displayed. Advertisements of the day, typography from the last century, and other tidbits that would add to the overall impression of the time in which the article existed. Will we lose this value on the Web? Pages created just five years ago already fail to render in today's browsers, as old HTML elements become deprecated in new standards. The advent of Object-Oriented Publishing takes this even further, separating not only content from its presentation, but its historical context as well. It's a tenuous balance between the efficiency of dynamic publishing and the value of learning from our past mistakes and achievements.

Regardless, be sure to take screenshots of all your work, which will always depict your designs accurately.

A Changing Process

It took us a while at *Wired* to fully embrace a process like
the one I've described above. Some designers found it
insulting to think that each and every story in a Web site
should be absolutely identical. Content should be designed
based on what it says and what it means. Visual design
communicates as well as the words, they would argue. And
I would agree, but there is a reality on the Web that forces
a compromise.

First, design can and should conform to content, but
tools are tools. We spent an entire chapter in this book discussing how consistency in user interface leads to building
context. Users learn how interfaces work, and expect those
interfaces to work the same time after time. Developing
custom design treatments for story after story on a Web site
can lead to a disorientation as users are forced to pick out
the particular useful bits of an interface over and over again
as they move through a site.

But more importantly, a dynamic publishing system can
give commercial Web sites an edge to survival. The Web is
still young, and business models are evolving as quickly as the
technology behind today's Web sites. Yet despite the surge in
"dot-com" stock prices and seemingly endless venture capital
being invested in startups, the fact remains that it can be
very difficult to provide free content supported with advertising. The cost of advertising on a Web site is significantly less
than what it costs to run ads in printed publications or on
television—two other forms of media that are typically free
to end users, with costs being offset by messages from sponsors. Ultimately, successful business models will emerge from
the chaos that is today's adolescent Web. But today, commercial sites need every edge they can muster.

The same held true for the evolving content development process we experimented with at HotWired over the
first few years of our existence. Since we came from *Wired*
magazine, we followed a traditional print publishing
process—it was what we knew. It was a linear process. Step
by step we worked on individual pieces of content until

they were ultimately published on our Web site. If you were
to chart how it worked, it would have looked something
like the diagram to the right.

Using this method, an author
would iterate with an editor on the
particular story until they were both
satisfied with the content. Then, an
editor would send the finished piece to
a copy editor, who would go over the
work in detail, checking grammar,
spelling, and facts, as well as ensuring
everything was in compliance with our
editorial style guidelines. From there,
the story would move into production,
where HTML specialists would add
the basic tags: paragraphs and links,
plus standard navigation like headers
and footers. Production would send
the story to a designer, who would do a
complete treatment on the piece—
much like a feature in a magazine.

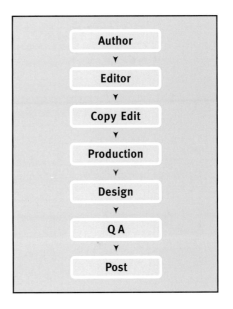

Illustrations and photography would be commissioned; colors, type and layout would be developed; display copy would
be created. Production and even copy editing steps would
often be repeated here to ensure nothing was changed.
Then, to the Quality Assurance (QA) people, who would
test the new content in a variety of browsers and ensure
that standards for page performance and server compatibility were maintained. Finally, the story would be posted by
the webmaster, the one responsible for the live site. With
such an elaborate process, it won't come as a surprise that
we weren't able to publish very much. With a dozen sections in our site, we added only a story or two to each section in a week. Lots of content compared to a print magazine, but not nearly enough for a Web site.

The Object-Oriented Publishing process changed all of
that. The new system essentially split the staff into two

groups: those who developed the system, and those who operated it.

Now, the process looked like this: Authors and editors continued to collaborate and iterate the stories, and copy editors continued their rigorous inspection. But now, after a production manager had created the basic HTML paragraphs and links, the content was added to the database and

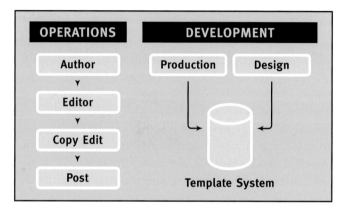

was ready for publishing. At the same time, designers and engineers were collaborating on template systems similar to the one we looked at previously in this chapter. They would blend the interface with the procedural code applicable to all the content being fed into the database by editors. Designers could focus on macro issues like site architecture, and micro issues like search interfaces and headline rendering and be assured of consistency throughout the sites. The content would simply flow into the right places and the site would be alive.

Everyone could focus their energies on developing more and better Web sites. We could keep up with falling advertising rates without resorting to an ever-expanding staff. Dynamic publishing systems can pay off in untold ways.

The Dangers of Being Dynamic

Admittedly, I am ever an optimist. The scenario I've deconstructed in this chapter is a relatively simple one. An ever-growing commercial Web site would undoubtedly scale out of control without careful and frequent planning and revision. Still, a dynamic publishing system is a critical tool in keeping up with the hyperspeed growth of the Web. It frees designers and developers from the tyranny of mindless maintenance and updates, allowing them to focus on creating more useful and engaging sites. Think of the process as a design amplifier: It gives you the ability to do more and better work.

That is not to say that dynamic publishing is without its flaws. I've stated over and over in this book that HTML is simple, and it is. So are the scripting languages behind Object-Oriented Publishing—to a point. The scripts I've shared with you in the preceding examples are far from robust enough to survive in an actual highly trafficked Web site. They lack the complexity of checking for errors, nor are they optimized for efficiency—they are designed to illustrate the concepts behind dynamic publishing.

The added complexity of building pages as collections of server-side scripts requires a much more developed level of collaboration among your Web team. Our conceptual triangle of Structure, Behavior, and Presentation is more at work now than ever before. Engineers, designers, and editors must be completely synchronized. Everyone must understand how the system works and what exactly his or her role in the process is. Without this understanding, templates, interfaces, and content repositories simply cannot function.

Another warning: Dynamic publishing systems can make you lazy. Many of the benefits I've outlined here can make the workflow behind a Web site much more efficient. It is critical to remember to keep quality checks in place as the pace of publishing increases. When a system is designed to let anyone publish anything at any time, the possibility that something can go wrong increases exponentially.

Take, for example, this excerpt from a page on the Excite portal. The Daily News page on Excite is a wonder of dynamic publishing. Hundreds of stories a day are aggregated from dozens of news sources to give readers access to more information than any printed source could ever hope to do. Personalization tools allow users to create custom views of news that interest them. It's a very powerful application indeed.

Ongoing Coverage

Oddly Enough
Africa Embassy Bombs
Apple's New iMac

Astrology & Horoscopes
Astronomy News
Balloonist's Adventure

Capitol Hill Shooting
Celebrity Gossip
Clinton Sex Scandal

Crime & Criminals
Litigation & Lawsuits
Microsoft Fights DOJ

While it certainly would be odd for the African Embassy to bomb Apple's iMac—that's probably not what the editors had in mind.

Yet with all this power, it's easy to lose sight of the editorial heuristics on which professional publishers depend. This example shows a classic problem with dynamic publishing. Three headlines, probably all edited and chosen by smart editors, have been aggregated in a way that borders on the absurd. Simple copy editing would help here. The designers could have used bullets on each headline to distinguish them. The point is that dynamic publishing can lead to unforeseen mistakes if you're not very careful to keep things under control.

Design in an Object-Oriented World

What are the implications for designing within database-driven, dynamic Web sites? Think back to our discussion of client-side behavior in Chapter Four. It showed how using simple scripts in the browser can make an interface respond to the unknown variables in which our pages can exist. Page columns need to be flexible to accommodate different screen resolutions. Headlines can size themselves based on the width of a browser window. Typography becomes a game of guesswork against an unidentified selection of installed fonts.

Think also of our discussion of structure. If Object-Oriented Publishing teaches us anything, it is that good design comes from good planning. My simple example of a sermon archive would never have been successful had I not taken the time to fully understand the structure and ultimate architecture of the content. In Chapter Three we covered good Information Architecture coming from the patterns already present in content. In this chapter, I made explicit use of those patterns by infusing them in database structures and logical page templates.

This chapter offered tools for designers facing the uncertain future of dynamic design. We've left behind the absolutes of traditional graphic design. We're embracing a world of variables and uncertainty. The only way to thrive in such a nebulous environment is to start simply. Look for patterns. Build with little blocks into complex structures. Account for the limitations of the Web, the browsers, and the rich and diverse audience that will soon be flowing through your pages.

Now get busy. We've got a lot of work to do.

Index